THE SURVIVORS

THE SURVIVORS
A study of homeless young newcomers to London and the responses made to them

D. Brandon, K. Wells, C. Francis, E. Ramsay

Routledge & Kegan Paul
London, Boston and Henley

First published in 1980
by Routledge & Kegan Paul Ltd
39 Store Street,
London WC1E 7DD,
9 Park Street,
Boston, Mass. 02108, USA and
Broadway House,
Newtown Road,
Henley-on-Thames,
Oxon RG9 1EN
Printed in Great Britain by
Redwood Burn Limited
Trowbridge and Esher

British Library Cataloguing in Publication Data

The survivors.
  1. Youth - England - London metropolitan
  area
  2. Homelessness - England - London metropolitan
  area
  I. Brandon, David
  362.7   HQ799.G7   80-40170

ISBN 0 7100 0468 0

CONTENTS

AUTHORS' NOTE

The research described in this book was financed by the Department of Health and Social Security. The views expressed, together with the recommendations made, are not necessarily those of the Department of Health and Social Security or any other Government department.

PREFACE

This report represents a long and difficult journey,
financed by the DHSS, which could not have been completed
without the help of many people.   We would like to thank
David Fruin, Tilda Goldberg (both formerly of the
National Institute of Social Work); Jenny Clark, Kate
Hodgetts (former secretaries); Bryan Tully; Mary Bruce
(formerly of the DHSS);   June Lightfoot and Nick Beacock
(Campaign for the Homeless and Rootless (CHAR));   and many
workers at Centrepoint, North and the West End Reception
Centre, New Horizon Soho Project and scores of other
agencies.   We thank especially those 107 young men and
women who became our subjects and apologise for over-
simplifying their perspectives.   Our thanks to Shirley
Lightfoot who typed the manuscript.

Chapter 1

HOMELESS YOUNG PEOPLE

We have been studying the experiences and views of just
over one hundred 'homeless young newcomers to London'.
These came from a wide range of backgrounds and diverse
regions of the United Kingdom and Eire.   We selected them
during 1974 and early 1975, from among the users of three
projects offering emergency accommodation.   We interviewed them in depth and also, where possible, followed
them up at least one year later for a further interview.

We have also focused on those who define and respond to
the 'problem' or 'problems' these young people are supposed to present.   In particular, we have looked at the
various ways in which they are seen and responded to by
the host of agencies that cater primarily or incidentally
for the young homeless in London.   We begin with the
pressing question: how has the term 'homeless' been used
and who uses it about whom?

Homelessness among young people is no new social problem.   The plight of the 'outcast city arabs' was a major
stimulus to social concern in the mid-nineteenth century.
That concern played a substantial role in the drafting of
the early Lodging House Acts of 1851 and 1853 as well as
in the passing of the Forster (compulsory) Education Act
of 1870. (1)

In 1848, Shaftesbury and others observed more than
'30,000 naked, filthy, roaming, lawless and deserted children, quite distinct from the ordinary poor' in the London
area alone. (2)   An examination of 1,600 of these 'street
arabs' found that 116 had run away from home;   162 had had
several periods of imprisonment;   170 slept in lodging
houses;   219 had never slept in beds;   306 had lost either
one or both parents. (3)   Few social campaigners shared
the smug view of William Chance, stern advocate of Poor
Law policies in the 1890s - 'Vagrancy has flourished in
this country from the earliest times, and will probably

continue to flourish to the end of all time. The life
has many attractions, and is suited to our islanders' love
of travel and adventure.' (4)

Charles Trevelyan of the Charity Organisation Society
(1870) wrote about the chaotic growth of night shelters
and hostels to cater for those sleeping rough: (5)

> The London predatory class pass from casual wards to
> night refuges, and from one night refuge to another;
> and the existence of this great proletarian class is in
> great degree owing to these institutions. These
> people are in a far better position than persons in the
> highest ranks of society, for however high a person may
> be, he has to defray, out of his income, whatever that
> may be, his expenses of living, and of meeting the var-
> ious claims incident to his social position; and what
> he can spend on pleasure depends upon what is left
> after all other claims have been satisfied. But not
> so this predatory class of people - nothing, in short
> to divert them from indulgence in the merest sensual
> and criminal pleasures.

The notion of two classes of destitution - the 'deserving' and the 'undeserving' - was a powerful force in the
formulation of both nineteenth- and twentieth-century
social policies. Charles Booth in studying lodging-house
inhabitants divided them between the 'work-shy' and the
'poor derelicts of humanity'. (6) The former were harsh-
ly driven into work whilst the latter lived their lives
interchangeably between common lodging, casual ward, night
shelter and the workhouse. The famous Goschen minute
(1869), named after the then President of the Poor Law
Board, recommended to the Poor Law guardians that they
deal with the 'undeserving' whilst the 'deserving destitute' be referred to the Charity Organisation Society.

What kind of reception they were to receive from the
COS, the forerunner of modern social work, was evident
from the COS Review: (7)

> There can be no doubt that the poverty of the working
> class is due, not to their circumstances (which are
> more favourable than those of any other working popula-
> tion of Europe); but to their own improvident habits
> and thriftlessness. If they are ever to be more
> prosperous, it must be through self-denial, temperance
> and fore-thought.

Even though COS pioneers might admit the existence of
structural and social inequalities, the moral problem was

paramount.   'The people's houses are bad, because they
are badly built and arranged;   they are tenfold worse because the tenants' habits and lives are what they are.
Transplant them tomorrow to healthy and commodious houses,
and they would pollute and destroy them.' (8)

This general mix of socio-economic factors and a large
degree of moralising became more sophisticated in the
twentieth century.   At the height of the great economic
and industrial depression (1931) Frank Gray, keen observer
of homelessness, wrote: (9)

> Youth on the road has little to do with the unemployed
> situation in England.   It is true that a number of
> boys now on the road come from distressed areas, the
> coalfields of Durham and South Wales.   They are boys
> many of whom at the age of eighteen have never had work
> since leaving school, and have taken to the road in a
> spirit of desperation, made the keener by watching the
> distress of their parents, who themselves are also
> without employment;   but this element leaves the exis-
> tence of a much larger proportion of boy vagrants en-
> tirely unexplained.   Probably the most important con-
> tribution factor in the presence in the post-war period
> of large numbers of boys on the road, in the casual
> wards, and ultimately in our prisons, is the attitude
> of the mind of youth towards the realities of life.
> Young men of today, those particularly between the ages
> of 16 and 26, appear to lack stability and purpose in
> life and are irresponsible and casual, and above all
> are hostile to the slow and difficult steps which alone
> make for success.

Gray introduced the important notion of psychiatric and
intellectual handicap - 'A very large proportion indeed of
boys upon the road are mentally "peculiar", indeed if they
were not they would not be on the road'. (10)

Gray's theme was echoed more recently by the founder of
the Simon Community, the late Anton Wallich-Clifford
(1976).   'In the past, homelessness and poverty went
hand-in-hand;   today homelessness is more the product of
spiritual poverty than of material need'. (11)   Other
observers are even more critical of homeless people.
Stuart Whiteley wrote 'to his environment, the down and
out contributes nothing.   To exist in it he must be as
psychopathic as his neighbour'. (12)   Howard Bahr commented (13)

> The Skid Row man is or is perceived as being, defective
> physically (scarred, handicapped, aged and diseased),

mentally (psychotic, senile or manifesting bizarre
symptoms), morally (a pervert, criminal or addict),
psychologically (low esteem, high self aggression),
socially disaffiliated, legally (treated by the police
and courts as a resident of an occupied country rather
than as a free man), economically (impoverished, unemployed) and ecologically (as resident in a neighbour-
hood in which no 'decent' person would live).

These quotations see homeless people as a great, homo-
geneous defective lump - young and old alike.   It is only
in recent years that some agencies and observers have
become worried about this stereotyping.   Among these is
New Horizon, a day centre for homeless young people:

By the very nature of our work we are going to meet
people who are more damaged than most through their
extreme experiences, but we recognise that drawing
attention to such emotive subjects can lead to a situation where all homeless people become tarred with the
label 'drifter' or 'dosser' such that there is no
allocation of funds and people, which might have pre-
vented their drift into this lifestyle in the first
place. (14)

Many (clients) have been stigmatised by labels and now
view themselves with the impersonality and coldness the
labels suggest: failures, junkies, criminals. (15)

Clashing definitions make the whole question of numbers
of young homeless people a minefield.   Gillian Diamond
defines a person as homeless (16)

when he or she has no place where he has the right to
sleep.   This includes not only those who are literally
out on the streets, but also those sleeping in derelict
houses, unauthorised squatters, people in bed and
breakfast hotels and short stay hostels and people
crashing on friends' floors or doubling up with relatives.

Much more subjective and expansionist is Margaret Norris'
attempt - 'Homeless is to include any state where the
present accommodation was inadequate for reasons which
seemed good to the applicant.' (17)
Theodore Caplow's sociological definition gives the
accommodation ingredient a peripheral place.   'Homelessness is a condition of detachment from society character-
ised by the absence or attenuation of the affiliative

bonds that link settled persons to a network of intercon-
nected social structures'. (18)   Attempts to widen the
definition, like those of Norris and Caplow, although influential, have had stout opponents.   Peter Beresford
comments tersely:'the use of the term "single homelessness" should be restricted to its face value meaning, to
cover those who are actually homeless.' (19)

Presumably the Departments of Environment and Health
and Social Security would have his support for their definition - 'those who have no roof or who appear likely to
lose their shelter within a month ...' (20) although
Rosamunde Blackler would exclude young people actually
homeless in London but who have homes elsewhere.   'Our
own experience is that the estimated figure of 10,000
young homeless in London is needlessly inflated by the inclusion of hundreds of boys and girls who, in fact, have
a bed waiting for them somewhere'. (21)

Far from reflecting a systematic attempt to lasso a
social phenomenon out there, the term homeless reflects
mainly the views of those who have been responsible for,
or influenced the making of social policy over the centuries.   The voice of the defined has rarely been heard.

Definition debates echo the beliefs of important
people making pronouncements about the very poor.   To
adapt Barbara Ward's phrase - the process reflects the
views of those whose plans have worked out talking of
those whose plans have not. (22)   Perhaps the medieval
poem 'Piers Plowman' has the most succinct comment:

But beggars about midsummer go breadless to supper,
And winter is worse, for they are wet-shod wanderers
Frozen and famished and foully challenged
And berated by rich men so that it is rueful to listen.

More precisely, the debates echo a perceived need to do
something about people without homes; to stir public con-
science by gaining attention and media time.   'Homeless
people are perceived as presenting a definite social problem to the potential providers and solvers.   'Homeless'
connects with certain anxieties, worries, anger and even
hot moral indignation about the lack of, or even surplus
of, various projects like night shelters, hostels, day
centres and ordinary housing provision.   Necessarily,
then, the term is more informative about those who use it
rather than those of whom it is used.   More neutral terms
like homeless have tended to replace those like 'unclub-
bable', 'drifter', 'socially inadequate' or 'sociopath'
which imply moral positions.

We have taken homeless to mean using emergency accommo-

dation, including sleeping rough, bed-and-breakfast, cheap
hotels, squats, sleeping on floors, night shelters, reception centres and a variety of short stay hostels.   We
have focused on migrants who had very recently arrived in
London, were under twenty-six years old and were using
three particular projects offering short stay or emergency
accommodation.   (These, referred to as 'the selected projects', were Centrepoint, The West End Reception Centre
(both in Soho), and North (in Highgate).)

Although there has been a great quantity of research
into older homeless people, (23) variously described as
vagrants, tramps and dossers, little is known about the
homeless young.   This lack of evidence seemed no deter-
rent to numerous dogmatic, sometimes even wildly imaginative statements, particularly about the size and scale of
the problem.   One of the few serious studies in this
field was that of Gill Diamond at Centrepoint. (24)   However we were sceptical of the results of this study which
appeared to show a more 'normal' population than expected.
We wanted to do research which validated the information
given by subjects as we suspected there was a great deal
of misinformation.

Much information from voluntary agencies is blurred by
the snapshot effect.   Young people drift into London from
the provinces and are handled by a variety of agencies for
a few days or weeks;   a few become West End regulars,
living or hanging around the central city area.   The
latter tend to have a disproportionate impact on the image
of the young homeless person.   In assessing their
clients, agencies often make insufficient allowance for
the role they play in affecting a client's behaviour and,
in particular, the way in which he presents himself to
them.   Nor do they adequately allow for the extreme and
usually episodic nature of the homeless experience, which
is rarely typical of the contexts in which the client has
and will spend most of his life.   We wanted to set our
subjects' experiences in London in a long-term and broader
perspective.   We delved into their backgrounds and personalities and tried to pierce beneath appearances.   We
managed to follow up and re-interview 42 per cent of the
sample a year or so later.

In our research, we have preferred to see homelessness
among young people as revolving around four major elements
- housing, mobility, employment and social processing (in
social work, criminal and psychiatric settings etc.).
These were seen as being played out against a background
of particular social and individual meanings.   We wanted
to stress the qualities of survival and self-realisation
which extreme forms of social and economic deprivation can

bring out or dampen down.   How would these young people
survive both in a material and psychological sense?
Apart from simply surviving, how might they extend and
fulfil themselves through their experiences of migration
and homelessness?

Although David Eversley argued recently that we are
substantially better housed than a decade or two ago,
there are still considerable areas of homelessness particularly in the large cities. (25)   In Britain the broad
choice is now between home ownership and council housing
with the privately rented sector declining year by year.
Little housing is presently available for single people
with low income.   In the 1971 census only 6 per cent of
the England and Wales housing stock consisted of one- or
two-room dwellings.   Most local authorities have, until
very recently, steadfastly refused to accept applications
for housing from those who are single and under thirty.
Obtaining mortgages may also be difficult. (26)

There is now less cheap communal accommodation for the
migrant newcomer to most of our large cities.   The total
stock of hostel and lodging-house accommodation declined
by 17 per cent between 1965 and 1972.   There were 37,845
beds in 1965 Britain and only 31,253 seven years later.
The greatest loss had been in Scotland, where about one-
third of the total of beds had disappeared, whilst London
lost 13 per cent during the same period. (27)

Great pressure has been put on cheap accommodation,
flats, bed-sits and lodgings by the rapid expansion in the
student population.   Students are generally more effective than other young people in competing for scarce resources. (28)   The Chief Executive of Brighton commenting
on the plans for expanding the University of Sussex from
4,000 to 6,000 by 1982 said - 'unless action is taken, the
projected expansion of the University will worsen the already intolerably difficult housing situation for the
town'. (29)

Between 1966 and 1971, a period in which all single
households grew by 30 per cent and all flat-sharings by 20
per cent, the growth among the under-thirties was 81 per
cent and 66 per cent respectively. (30)   A Department of
the Environment study (1971) showed that increasing numbers of young people were anxious to obtain independent,
self-contained accommodation. (31)   About this process
Joan Clegg observed, 'we now have to take into account
that for many there may be a transitional stage of living
separately from parents which is described as "living away
from home"; that is, the accommodation currently occupied
is seen as fulfilling a need to be independent but is not
yet expressed as "setting up home".' (32)

The London Boroughs' Association put all these elements
rather soberly in a recent report: (33)

It is not surprising that the information collected
makes it clear that there is an increasing proportion
of single people in the London population; that the
commonly-held view that single people do not encounter
financial difficulties in housing themselves is incor-
rect; that the combined effect of local authority
policies (such as clearance and municipalisation) and
of changes in the private sector (such as the declining
availability of accommodation to rent and the closure
of common lodging houses and changes in policy by certain voluntary bodies which have excluded their former
clientele) has been to reduce the accommodation available to single people; and that a very severe degree
of hardship is encountered by many single people as a
result of housing difficulties.

The second element is geographical mobility. Not only
are large numbers of young people wanting to leave the
family home before settling down, usually in marriage and
the raising of a family, but many, as for centuries, move
to other parts of the country.
Figures on the mobility of young people are difficult
to find.   Table 1.1 gives some details from 1971 Census
of migrants in the various age groups moving into the
Greater London area.

TABLE 1.1 Migrants moving into GLC area within one year
preceding the 1971 Census by sex, age and marital
condition (10 per cent sample)

Age last birthday	Males			Females		
	Total	Single	Married	Total	Single	Married
15-19	660	636	24	967	800	167
20-4	2071	1462	601	2345	1384	953
25-9	1097	467	607	913	277	612
All ages	6905	3961	2727	7128	3780	2880

Source: Census 1971, 'Migration Regional Report South
East Region Part 1', p. 85.

The figures in Table 1.2 are based on a 10 per cent
sample asked whether their usual address in London at the
time of the census differed from their usual address a
year earlier, and if so, where they had been then.   The

TABLE 1.2   Migrants into GLC area within one year preceding census by area of former usual residence (10 per cent sample)

Area of former residence	Males				Females			
	15-19	20-4	25-9	All ages 1+ over	15-19	20-4	25-9	All ages 1+ over
ENGLAND:								
North	34	102	44	281	42	86	33	249
Yorkshire and Humberside	40	144	51	374	71	175	41	412
North-west	48	187	75	538	59	187	66	514
East Midlands	37	89	41	275	43	103	35	277
West Midlands	40	142	64	414	62	138	57	377
East Anglia	24	95	38	269	32	92	39	284
South-east (excl. GLC)	289	877	564	3489	485	1074	503	3884
South-west	66	163	91	541	85	227	60	584
WALES	29	109	44	251	31	103	21	226
SCOTLAND	53	163	85	473	57	160	58	421
N. IRELAND	19	35	19	120	18	35	16	108
EIRE	44	144	80	374	84	134	64	361
CHANNEL ISLES AND I. OF MAN	4	14	8	37	8	15	9	45
Total	727	2264	1204	7436	1077	2529	1002	7642

Source: 'Migration Regional Report South East Region Part 1', p. 20.

figures apply only to people actually resident in the GLC
area at the time of the census.   It would cover the homeless very inadequately.   The Office of Population and
Census Surveys calculate the sampling error as n x 0.9.

The numbers of males and females are roughly similar.
Numbers from the south-east (excluding the GLC) are high
at about 50 per cent of the total, whereas Scotland provides a relatively small proportion.   More of the women
are married.   The figures for those in the GLC area at
the time of the census but actually resident elsewhere
are: Males 34,425, Females 34,180 (all ages).

Such mobility can be socially stigmatised.   Whilst
movement among student groups and young people entering
nursing careers has long been acceptable, mobility among
working-class youngsters is often viewed as 'just drifting' and a way of avoiding responsibilities - a modern
equivalent of 'running away to sea'.

The Vagrancy Acts actively discriminate against those
of all ages 'wandering abroad' and this can mean fines and
even short periods of imprisonment.   It can actually be
difficult for young people to get financial help.   A
recent report stated that 'homeless people often receive
unsympathetic treatment by DHSS officials who regard their
circumstances as "suspicious" and their needs as having
low priority.' (34)

Young people are often moving away from areas of high
unemployment.   Few have relevant skills and education to
compete for existing job opportunities: (35)

Yet the new work tends to take place in centre-cities
with a high concentration of business head-quarters or
on fresh sites away from the older industrial areas.
This introduces in city after city a mismatch between
work and residence, since the more skilled operators
are often the children and grandchildren of those who
escaped to nineteenth century suburbia.   The less
skilled workers can find themselves in run down centre-
city housing in areas from which the jobs are draining
away.

Young people generally find it hard to compete for
existing jobs.   The July 1976 unemployment rates for
workers under twenty-five, excluding school-leavers, were
10 per cent for males and 7.3 per cent for females, nearly
twice that of other age groups in Great Britain. (36)   In
January 1974 there were 0.27 unemployed young people for
every vacancy at the Careers Office;   by January 1977 that
figure had increased to 6.01 young people. (37)

Disproportionate increases in unemployment among young

people are associated with the declining demand for manual labour and strict limits on new recruitment resulting from the industrial recession. Homeless young people are competing for a variety of jobs, but mainly in the catering, building and tourist industries. The problems sometimes begin when work is found. 'Many homeless, particularly those working in catering, are sent to jobs paying less than the legal minimum of pay and involve working in appalling conditions.' (38)

For some minority groups the situation is worse. Not only are West Indian children brought up in inferior housing conditions, frequently with severe overcrowding, but they have a much higher unemployment rate after leaving school. (39) Unemployment among the various ethnic minorities in the EEC rose by 110 per cent for males and 275 per cent for females between February 1975 and February 1976. (40)

Little is known about either the physical or psychiatric health of young homeless people. To what extent does poor physical or psychiatric health contribute to homelessness? Are there physical and psychiatric costs in the homeless life-style? Drug overdosing, VD, and infestation cause problems in an environment where medical care is grossly inadequate. Many hostels find it difficult to get adequate general practitioner coverage. (41) Only 40 per cent of the estimated population of single homeless in Liverpool were registered with a GP at any one time. (42)

Wingfield Digby's comprehensive survey of hostels and lodging houses showed that young men are more than twice as likely to have been hospital inpatients within the previous three months than the average for their group in the general population. (43) Joy Holloway's study of 25 homeless men under thirty years old in Leeds suggested that 80 per cent had an obvious 'mental disorder' even though only five had ever seen a psychiatrist. Six of the men had had serious illnesses in childhood although none had a serious physical handicap. Half had had prison sentences and all but six some trouble with the police as adults. Nine were classified as drinking heavily and a further six as very heavily. (44)

Homeless young people are variously defined with either the lack of accommodation or deficiencies in social relationships as the central focus. Some observers have tended to stress character deficiencies, particularly in the last century; some draw attention to accommodation and employment contractions. In our view, these people are the most visible segment of a substantial number of the young quite ordinarily leaving home, seeking work and extending their personal and social experience.

One crucial element, infrequently studied, is the world
of the helper - for instance, the worker in the night
shelter or advice centre, the political campaigner.   They
seem to share a fundamental pessimism about the nature of
homelessness.   'Homeless people' are directed and controlled in various ways by representatives of a respectable society perceiving its values as superior to, and
quite different from theirs.   'The defectives are now
stigmatised not only by community definition but by the
professional experts' ideas about the nature of their
defectiveness.   The experts' theories about the nature of
stigmatisation and the attempted operationalisation of
those theories by the clinicians, have become critical
determinants of the self concept of the individual being
rehabilitated and of society's reaction to him.' (45)

Chapter 2

THE HOMELESS SCENE

In this chapter, we continue to outline the background to
our research by looking first at the people and settings
that make up the 'homeless scene' and then at various
popular conceptions of it.   Our main concern is with the
settings in which homeless young newcomers are to be found
and, in particular, with the three projects at which we
selected our sample.

THE HOMELESS SCENE: PEOPLE AND PLACES

Whatever the agreed definition, homeless people constitute
only a tiny minority of immigrants into London.   Considerable evidence also indicates that substantial proportions of the homeless are either indigenous to the capital
or over twenty-six years old. (1)
   On any one night, the London homeless population is in
many different settings; some very difficult to locate
and enumerate.   Some sleep rough in rail stations, on
park benches, in derelict houses, launderettes and public
toilets.   Others reside in the declining numbers of
lodging houses; in reception centres, hostels, night
shelters and cheap bed-and-breakfast places; yet others
are serving periods in prison, often for drunkenness
offences or breaches of the Vagrancy Acts or presently re-
siding in general or mental hospitals. (2)
   Some of the young people with whom this study is concerned arrive at railway stations; others come via bus or
hitchhiking into the city centre.   Many are soon staying
in one of our three selected projects - Centrepoint, WERC
(West End Reception Centre) and North.   But many others
are staying in the dozens of other projects and even
wandering the streets or in the various homeless settings
outlined.   Most of these youngsters are staying in

various kinds of emergency accommodation for several days or weeks and then moving on.   This vast circulation process probably encompasses several thousand young
people at least in the course of one year.   Some stay for
a night or two;   others for several months or even years.
The very young, running away from home and school, tend to
be picked up reasonably speedily and returned home by the
police or social services.   One fourteen-year-old was
flown back to Glasgow twice in one week by one local
authority.

It is useful to identify various groups of homeless
young people in London although there is a great deal of
permeation between the groups.   There are the new arrivals, the major concern of our study, who have been on the
circuit for less than a few months and either leave or
gradually merge into the long-termers who are, in central
London anyway, called West End regulars.   Some of these
may have been on the Piccadilly scene for years and may
have links with the buying and selling of various kinds
of drugs.   Another group are the local homeless who are
not nearly so visible, but who form a sizeable segment of
the homeless population.   They tend to disappear into
the homes of relatives or friends or stay with a succession of contacts.   Recent shortages of cheap hotel and
hostel accommodation push numbers of tourists into the
homeless circuit.

The homeless scene consists of various kinds of settings both intended and unintended.   There is formal and
intentional provision in the shape of statutory, voluntary, commercial and private organisations catering for
groups which include the homeless.   Much of this accommodation is of poor quality. (3)   Homeless young people
share the scene with older and more regular users, although old and young tend to be distributed differently.
This is particularly so in the statutory and voluntary
society sectors.

Statutory facilities - Reception centres, social security
offices, employment exchanges, local authority children's
homes, social service offices, probation hostels and
fieldwork services, a variety of day centres and advice
centres, prisons, psychiatric services, resettlement
centres.

Voluntary societies - Wide range of hostels, night shelters, longer term homes, day centres, soup runs, advice
facilities, detached youth workers, counselling services;
co-ordinating bodies like CHAR, Crisis at Christmas, Con-
sortium, SCODA (drug dependency), No Fixed Abode (East End

of London);   and referral agencies like After Six and the
National Association of Voluntary Hostels.

Commercial organisations - Lodging houses and hostels;
bed-and-breakfast places, employment and accommodation
agencies.

Ad hoc (unintended) - Rail and bus stations, cinemas, tube
trains, launderettes, park benches, toilets, hotel heating
grids, squatting, amusement arcades, derelict houses,
clubs, all-night cafés, casual contacts.

The most important source of information about lodging
houses and related kinds of hostels is the Wingfield Digby
report.   This shows that between 1965 and 1972 there was
a 13 per cent decline in the number of beds in this kind
of accommodation within the GLC area. (4)   By 1972, there
were 10,613 beds (8,517 in all-male hostels, 1,102 in all-
female ones and 994 in mixed ones), comprising 34 per cent
of the total national provision. (5)   Table 2.1 shows the
organisations which provided these beds.

TABLE 2.1 Numbers of beds in lodging houses and related
kinds of hostels in GLC area, 1972, according to source of
supply

Organisation	No. of beds
Local authorities	1,785
Salvation Army	2,548
Church Army	698
Other voluntary bodies	1,581
Private/commercial	1,610
Commercial organisations	2,391
Total	10,613

Nationally this study showed that in 1972 29 per cent of
male occupants were between the ages of fifteen and
twenty-nine compared with 10 per cent in the 1965
National Assistance Board study. (6)

Statutory provision

The only statutory residential provision for 'people
without a settled way of living' is reception centres,
children of the nineteenth-century casual wards. (7)   The
last seventy years has seen the development of the welfare

state and the gradual extension of state power into social problems.   Homelessness is unusual in experiencing a contradiction in statutory provision and the growing development of voluntary societies. (8)

There were eight centres in London during our study compared with twenty-eight in the 1920s.   Four take 'casual' users, those accommodated on a nightly basis. One centre is only for women and another has beds for both men and women.   Although the number of users varies widely from season to season the total bed capacity at that time (1974) for male casuals was 580 and 8 for female casuals;   614 for male residents and 60 for females.   The bulk of this provision was at the huge Camberwell centre. The West End Reception Centre admits younger homeless men only.   With this exception, proportions of young people in the centres are low.   Centres are considered damaging to the young.

Central government provides income support for the homeless through social security offices.   Discretionary emergency help is available to those without a settled address either through financial grant or by vouchers for lodging houses.

The role of local authorities with regard to homeless single people has been fairly restricted. (9)   In 1974 local social services authorities were no longer required to submit schemes (in respect of certain duties under the National Assistance Act 1948) to the Department of Health and Social Security for approval but the Secretary of State for Social Services issued a direction to those authorities to make arrangements to provide residential accommodation for those people in need of care and attention and temporary accommodation for people made homeless in unforeseen circumstances.

Some authorities provide lodging houses like Bruce House in Westminster.   The London Borough of Camden runs a night shelter, near Euston station.   Housing departments provide Housing Aid and Advice Centres and single people can be included on housing waiting lists although priority is still firmly given to families and the elderly.   The recent Housing (Homeless Persons) Act 1977 expands the responsibilities of local authorities in the area of single homelessness but young people as such are not included as a priority group in this legislation. (10) In the Code of Guidance to the Act, homeless single young people at risk are defined as a group to whom local authorities might decide to give priority as 'vulnerable for other special reasons'.

The most recent statutory development is a walk-in medical centre for young homeless in Soho.   This is to be

administered by the Area Health Authority and financed by
DHSS as a three-year experimental project. (11)
   Homeless people discharged from penal institutions come
under the care of the Probation and After Care service who
administer a number of hostels.   Hospitals, both general
and psychiatric, may reluctantly provide beds for people
who have really nowhere else to go. (12)   Most other institutions offering accommodation are staffed by untrained
and unqualified personnel.   The reception centres are run
by civil servants and centre assistants with a modest programme of in-service training and occasional external
seminars.   However the staff can call on a wide range of
different specialist advice if they consider it necessary.

Voluntary society provision

There are a wide range of different services provided by
voluntary societies in the London area.   The major
strategy of successive governments has been to finance the
development of voluntary bodies and co-ordinating organisations.   For example, 85 per cent of Christian Action's
budget on homelessness in 1974 came from central government sources.   Voluntary societies receive money through
a variety of channels including Urban Aid programmes, the
Supplementary Benefits Commission and the Housing Corporation.   The Wingfield Digby study showed that 4,827 beds
were provided in the GLC area by various voluntary societies.   More than half were administered by the Salvation
Army with the Church Army also a large provider.   The
founder of the Salvation Army, General Booth, was much
concerned with the destitute in London. (13)
   Most other organisations, like Dr Barnardo's and the
Shaftesbury Homes formed in the nineteenth century, and
inspired by the plight of homeless youth and children,
have long ago moved into longer-term and preventive work.
They were replaced by successive waves of newer and
smaller organisations centring on social evangelists.
Perhaps the most important of these figures in the 1960s
was the late Anton Wallich-Clifford who founded the Simon
Community.   He established a chain of shelters and small
communities all over Britain which took 'social mis-
fits'. (14)
   In the early 1970s, the Cyrenians took over much of the
work and many projects and have now established themselves
in West London. (15)   The St Mungo's Community, important
to provision for older men, took over Simon's work in central London. (16)   They organise soup runs, shelters for
the homeless and a chain of projects for homeless men.

The rather sporadic and piecemeal development of projects specifically for young people led to large numbers
of small harassed agencies.   Many were responses to particular problems, like the development of the drug subcul-
ture in the late 1960s.   Broadly, voluntary society activity separates into three main functions: contact and
rescue; advice and direction; longer-term accommodation.
   Organisations like the Soho Project (17) employ detached youth workers wandering the Soho streets at night con-
tacting young drifters.   Before his imprisonment, Roger
Gleaves founded the Old Catholic Community Service and
rescued young boys from Euston Station, some of whom were
used for immoral purposes. (18)   The night shelters, Centrepoint, St Giles, Link, North, Roof and Rink (some now
closed), provide overnight emergency accommodation.
   These rescue organisations offer very short-term accommodation and pass people on to advice centres.   New Horizon provides good day centre facilities.   Nucleus provides advice and counselling for young people in the
Earl's Court area.   The Blenheim Project responded to the
needs of drifting youngsters in Notting Hill Gate. (19)
The Irish Centre and Benburb Base give advice to groups
from Ireland; (20)   the Royal Scottish Corporation, those
from Scotland.   The Irish Centre was particularly disturbed that newcomers 'robbed Ireland of its greatest wealth
- its own young people'. (21)   New Horizon pioneered an
analysis of why young Scots had left their home
country. (22)   GALS (Girls Alone in London Service) runs
a short-term hostel with an advice and counselling service. (23)
   Organisations have widely varying styles.   Some involve their residents in the daily running of projects
like the Camden Accommodation Scheme, whilst GALS runs on
a more maternalistic model.   Some have selection procedures which exclude many types of possible residents, like
the epileptic, enuretic, the potentially aggressive,
whilst others select positively and cater for specialist
groups like drug dependents or alcoholics. (24)

Commercial provision

Throughout this century, there has been a steep decline in
numbers of beds provided by commercial and private organisations.   The Metropolitan Police Commissioner reported
in 1889 that in his area there were one thousand lodging
houses, mostly commercial, with beds for 31,651. (25)
This is roughly equivalent to the present total number of
beds in hostels and lodging houses in the whole of

Britain.   Although there was a 34 per cent decline in
commercial provision between 1965 and 1972, roughly twice
the rate of decline in other sectors, these bodies still
provided about 40 per cent of the British total. (26)
   The giant provider in London was and is Rowton House
founded in the last decade of Victoriana.   They erected a
chain of working men's hostels which provided 3,700 beds
by 1903.   They had a philosophy of 'philanthropy at 5 per
cent' and three huge hostels still remain - Arlington
House (1,054 beds), Bondway (420 beds), and Tower House
(695 beds) and cost about £1 a night for a cubicle.
   Much of the remaining accommodation is in small hostels
which feel the impact of rising costs, improving fire
regulations and inner-city redevelopment programmes.
Most provision in the commercial sector is too expensive
for the homeless and usually rejects DHSS lodging
vouchers, expecting payment a week in advance.
   Homeless young people use a range of non-residential
commercial facilities including employment and accommodation agencies.   Peter Beresford analysed the closure of
cheap cafés because of 'rising food prices, increasing
overheads, heating, lights, rates, VAT and the money to be
made from selling out'. (27)   He comments that these
cafés offered homeless people an informal setting to come
in out of the cold, to make social contact, and to have a
cheap meal.

Ad hoc provision

'I live in Trafalgar Square with four lions to guard me'.
This old pre-First World War song catches some of the
pathos of sleeping rough in London.   The shelterless have
a long history in central London and have inspired paint-
ings, songs, films and the Vagrancy Acts of 1824, 1825 and
1935 as well as a wide range of voluntary societies like
the Salvation Army.
   Regular censuses have been completed in central London
since 1904, which discovered 1,797 people sleeping rough
and this included fifty children.   The 1910 survey
counted a peak of 2,730 men and women.   Although with the
war numbers diminished rapidly they climbed again in the
depression of the 1930s and the 1935 Vagrancy Act amended
the situation whereby sleeping rough itself had been an
offence.   Numbers declined again with the new war, but a
survey by the Salvation Army in 1962 discovered 72 people,
whilst National Association of Voluntary Hostels (recently
founded) was claiming 1,500 to 2,000 people sleeping rough
in London. (28)   Almost certainly this was an exaggera-
tion.

A National Assistance Board survey in 1965 found nearly
one thousand people sleeping rough in Britain;   28.6 per
cent were in the London area. (29)   They were mainly in
railway stations and parks.   In June 1971, a Christian
Action survey found 345 people sleeping rough in central
London;   112 completed questionnaires, many others being
asleep or very drunk.   One quarter were under twenty-six
and 10 per cent over sixty years old.   About a quarter
said they had been in London under four weeks, a half for
over a year.   A St Mungo's survey in October 1972 found
1,415 people sleeping rough in Westminster, Camden and
Southwark.

This is perhaps the hardest area of homelessness of
which to make accurate estimates.   People sleep in tube
trains, launderettes, toilets, squats, walk about at night
and sleep during the day, doze in cinemas and railway
stations, crash on people's floors.   Large areas of the
problem are hidden and difficult to calculate.   Crisis at
Christmas report in 1976 must take the homeless fiction
prize, however, with 'there are 8,000 young people sleeping rough in London alone'. (30)

THE THREE SELECTED PROJECTS

1   Centrepoint (1974-5)

Centrepoint defines its purpose as the provision of
advice, support and emergency accommodation for homeless
people who are new to and/or at risk in central London.
It is the largest night shelter for the young in Britain
and has the over-all aim of 'preventive intervention' -
to arrest the degenerative process accompanying destitution in the West End by receiving and redistributing newcomers.   There are an average of 5,000 nightly admissions yearly of about 2,500 different individuals - 90
per cent come from outside London.   The majority are
male, although the proportion of females is high.

The night shelter is in part of St Anne's Church
buildings, Soho.   At the time of the study, premises consisted of a basement area containing twenty bunk beds
(with sheets and blankets) and a large ground-floor room
including the office, a bar area where food (local res-
taurant left-overs) and drinks were served, with a space
for sitting and talking.   Since the study, the dormitory
has been segregated - females sleep in a ground-floor
room.   The decor is colourful and the atmosphere informal.

The shelter is staffed by four full-time social workers

and a team of volunteers.   Normally there is a worker on
each night, supported by four or five volunteers coming in
for one or two nights weekly.   Volunteers' duties include
serving the food and befriending clients, and picking up
information about their backgrounds.   Information harves-
ted is fed into the 'briefing session' when the clients
have gone to bed.

The regime at the time of our research stressed a befriending and welfare rights approach to the problems of
young people.   There was extensive information available
on various benefits and notes about both accommodation and
work.

Prospective clients were screened by the duty worker at
the outside gate in Shaftesbury Avenue.   To gain entry,
they normally had to be under twenty-five and destitute.
However, both in terms of admission and permitted length
of stay, the selection policy tended to favour those considered to be vulnerable ('at risk'), willing to make a
concerted effort to settle and help themselves and also
new to London.   Workers were keen to exclude those obviously on alcohol or drugs, the potentially disruptive or
corruptive and 'those on the con'.   Especially when busy,
workers were reluctant to admit males who were older or
accompanied by friends on the grounds that they were more
resilient.   Males turned away were usually referred to
WERC, only 500 yards away.

During our survey, Centrepoint was rationing clients to
a maximum of between one and four nights.   The average
length of stay was two nights.   Clients had to re-apply
each evening and on reaching the maximum were rarely admitted for the next few months.   Some individuals gained
extra time by giving false names and avoiding recognition.

Centrepoint is actually more selective than other similar projects whilst espousing a doctrine that 'we deal
with those rejected by other agencies'.   In 1974 2,329
individuals were turned away compared with the total of
5,574 admissions (as distinct from individual users).
Centrepoint's policy favoured our target population so
that the proportion of people eligible for our study who
were turned away was probably small.

The 1974 annual report gives as a reason for turning
people away as 'sometimes full up'.   Beds were rarely
fully occupied and more often refusal to admit was to
reduce staff stress.   There was a tendency to restrict
numbers to an optimum for effective help.   Centrepoint
had beds for up to twenty people during 1974 and 1975,
occupation rates in those years were 15.3 and 13.8.

Gill Diamond's 1970 study of Centrepoint compiled information from case records of some 2,000 users.   Record-

ing was extremely haphazard, but she identified seven
categories of young people: new arrivals (53 per cent of
total); out of town drifters (11 per cent); fringe members of West End scene (11 per cent); West End regulars
(5 per cent); those recently leaving London accommodation
(7 per cent) and those who were stranded (10 per cent).

She felt that Centrepoint had failed in its declared
attempt to 'be a bridge between the street and the statutory and voluntary agencies which can help'. This failure stemmed from lack of a systematic referral strategy:
large numbers were referred from other agencies to Centrepoint and only 15 per cent of clients were referred to
helping agencies from the night shelter. (31)

We interviewed our subjects in a private room at
Centrepoint. Even though we had formal permission to
interview and the active support of the current Director,
co-operation was hard to achieve. Some workers felt we
might bully or exploit clients. Our £1 interview fee was
seen as a bribe. Publically, it was alleged that we
might be more interested in academic games than the homeless young people themselves and breach the agreed confidentiality. Workers alleged that we were really 'spies
of the DHSS', 'human tape recorders', and our subjects
were viewed as 'victims of homeless research'.

2   West End Reception Centre (1974-5)

West End Reception Centre is responsible, along with other
centres under schedule 4 (2) of the Ministry of Social
Security Act 1966, for resettling those leading an unsettled way of life. The policy of WERC is to serve younger
homeless men who have drifted into the West End to seek
work. The maximum age for admission during our study was
forty, but this has been reduced to thirty-five. While
we interviewed, this tended to vary nightly so that older
people were not turned away while beds were empty.

The Centre is based in an old hospital just off Dean
Street, Soho, and has facilities for eighty men. There
are dormitories, a cafeteria and recreational facilities
including three TV rooms (one for the 'residents'), a
table tennis room and a darts room. Admission begins at
5 pm and continues until all beds are filled. Official
policy dictates that anyone who is destitute should be
admitted. Individuals should only be refused if they
were obviously drunk and disorderly. Anyone with more
than £1 was not considered destitute although admission
staff could consider charging for a bed. Persons under
seventeen are normally referred either to the social ser-

vices departments or the police.   Casuals are admitted on
a nightly basis and those considered in need of a more
protected environment may be offered 'resident' status.
Residents have a separate dormitory and can stay indoors
during the day with a midday meal whilst casuals have to
leave by 11 am.
     Rules are displayed in the waiting room.   These in-
clude no smoking in bed and not swearing;   consumers may
be banned for breaking them.   Clients are required to
provide information about any criminal record, work experience and history of physical or psychiatric illness.
They are required to shower under supervision and their
clothes are inspected for vermin.   Once admitted they may
not normally leave until 11 am the following morning after
completing some domestic task like washing the floor.
Those accepted as residents are given work around the
centre (where they have no outside employment) for which
they receive pocket money.
     Each person has a more detailed interview with a re-
settlement officer and is re-interviewed every three or
four days.   This ensures that he is seriously seeking
work.   Users may stay indefinitely provided they are
seeking employment but the average length of stay for
casuals was only 2.4 days.   People considered not serious
work-seekers are sent to 'No Fixed Abode' DHSS offices for
'a taste of reality' (the manager).   When they find a job
they may remain in the centre for the first few weeks, but
would be required to pay for their board and lodging.
     In general, the centre has a resettlement purpose and
is not for casual workers.   Regular employment is central
to an independent life in its philosophy and adequacy is
measured by employment prospects.   The centre guards
against being thought of as an 'easy touch' and tries to
prevent younger men from learning the tricks used by the
older men.   Daily 10 per cent checks are made with local
social security offices to ensure that double claims are
not made.   The manager believes that 30 per cent of men
are 'swinging the lead' and living on the cheap but the
majority are 'good lads' who need discipline and help to
get on their feet.   Various special services like the
provision of new clothing are available.
     The centre is staffed by four executive officers, four
clerical officers and one assistant, and four shifts of
four assistants dealing with admissions.   The staff
volunteer from the ranks of the civil service.   The
atmosphere is institutional, impersonal and formal;   admission staff are clearly distinguishable from users by
white overalls.   Whereas Centrepoint workers often have
degrees and in some cases are also professionally quali-

fied, the majority of centre assistants at this centre are
closer to the social and educational background of their
users.

We ordinarily selected our subjects in the centre waiting room and took them to our nearby office in Greek
Street.   WERC staff were always extremely helpful and co-
operative.   We were treated like the 'eyes of head
office' rather than as spies.   The manager wanted the
DHSS to appreciate more fully the nature and value of the
centre's role.

3   North

North was a short stay hostel in Highgate providing emergency accommodation and advice to young people aged
between 16-24, new to London and at risk.   It grew out of
the remnants of a previous project which had squatted in
the property and offered 'crash pad' accommodation.   It
was given short-life property status by Camden through
Student Community Housing and administered by the North
Camden Community Information Trust which was registered
with the Charity Commissioners.   There was a management
committee with six members including a local probation
officer.

The night shelter opened formally in July 1974.   It
was financed, in contrast to the large budgets of Centrepoint and WERC, by a weekly rent of £5 paid by residents
encouraged to sign on at the local employment exchange and
to claim supplementary benefit.   This source of money was
too irregular and inadequate to cover costs and applica-
tion was made to the Supplementary Benfits Commission who
refused a grant.   North, always struggling from one
crisis to another, folded about a year after inception.

Selection criteria were similar to Centrepoint but were
haphazardly applied.   Some users were over twenty-five
and others were arguably in no way at risk.   Length of
stay was initially two weeks, but became increasingly
flexible, some people staying over a month.   Clients were
formally required to bring a referral letter but this was
not often observed.

Premises were primitive with accommodation for ten individuals, consisting of mattresses on the floor and three
beds in one room on the ground floor.   There was a kitche
kitchen but no food was provided, the expectation being
that everyone would co-operate in making a meal.   The
whole atmosphere was informal, spontaneous and sometimes
volatile.   Some clients complained of drug-taking on the
premises.   The over-all aim of North was to create a

sense of community spirit and self-help in the house which
could assist people to become more settled.

The relationship between staff and clients was collu-
sive and fraternal.   The workers assumed a comradely or
brotherly approach in contrast to the maternal style of
Centrepoint and the paternalism of WERC.   Workers supported clients in squatting attempts.   They turned a blind
eye to their minor illegalities, and clients felt little
need to hold back incriminating information.   The staff
of two had simply turned their own homelessness into a
job.   Identification with clients was based on shared
experience rather than on a concern about the underdog as
at Centrepoint.

THE PUBLIC REALITY OF HOMELESSNESS

The drama of young homelessness not only involves clients,
the agencies and their sponsors but has become a public
spectacle.   Millions watch TV documentaries like 'Johnny
Go Home' and read newspaper articles, particularly at
Christmas time, and wonder why people become homeless and
who is to blame.

> Today, like any other day, about 200 children will run
> away from home.   Many of them will be teenage girls,
> and many of them will end up in Soho.   They are lured
> by the bright lights, but totally ignorant of the
> perils of the drug and sex pushers.   And they repre-
> sent one of the biggest social problems of the
> seventies (The 'Sun' - Tuesday, 6 February 1973).

> STARRY EYED YOUNGSTERS....   Children fleeing from an
> unhappy home, rebelling against boredom or simply
> lured by the bright lights are at risk of falling prey
> to every peril of London's underworld ('Evening Stan-
> dard' - 24 July 1975).

Often the media award romance tinged with horror to the
young homeless, and glamour to the project worker.   One
Centrepoint Director was described as 'SAVIOUR OF LONDON'S
LOST' ('Evening Standard', 27 April 1973).   Both workers
and young people play to this gallery.   Several subjects,
mostly females, attempted to provoke and shock both ourselves and our presumed audience with tales of tragedy,
abandon and deviant behaviour.   A few made references to
possible publicity.   For instance a female asked: 'Are
we going to be on TV?'.   A convicted rapist (who mono-
polised the interview with an exhaustive account of his

career of sexual deviation) said: 'I don't mind if it is used on TV or radio'.

While using the agencies, a surprisingly high proportion are liable to be questioned or at least observed by visiting social work students, researchers, journalists, TV teams, politicians and other dignitaries.   Centrepoint was deluged by requests from people 'to come and see for themselves'.   Large numbers of potential visitors were excluded and this policy undoubtedly influenced attitudes towards us.   There was the fear that outsiders might 'upset the delicate balance of the project', even to the point that it became a human menagerie.   Clients might feel intruded upon or alternatively attach glamour to being homeless.

The public image of homelessness may even actually encourage young people to try it.   Through the media and projects comes the message of tragedy, danger and harshness which may be translated into one of challenge, curiosity and glamour by young people.

Various popular stereotypes provide possible reference points for the homeless.   A few subjects dissociated themselves from 'homelessness' because of a link with hopelessness and inadequacy.   Some saw being homeless as a matter of personal responsibility or culpability; others claimed to be victims although that was less popular with them than with the workers.   Some claimed that homelessness was no problem and even to derive satisfaction from their ability to survive and prosper.   A few claimed that they were 'wanderers' and 'travellers' whilst one said he was enrolled in the 'University of the Road'. Generally, popular stereotypes provide a framework and vocabulary by which agencies relate to their public and the homeless relate to agencies.

Much of the energy of the voluntary agencies is directed towards campaigning and fund-raising.   They compete with other social causes and even among themselves for influence and resources.   To command attention, they often present an alarmist picture of the extent and dangers of homelessness.   The problem is packaged in black-and-white terms to ensure easy public assimilation and to provoke unambivalent feelings of anxiety, pathos and guilt.   Homeless young people are often exclusively depicted as victims of circumstance, as naive, deprived, disturbed and lonely youngsters, 'at risk' in a hostile and uncaring environment.   This results in an over negative picture of their situation and one that understates their capacities for survival, self-help and self-direction.

The media are the main mouthpiece of the agencies.

They usually faithfully reproduce the agencies' claims.
They also make use of similar motifs: for instance, im-
mature, impulsive youngsters, who are corruptible but
still reclaimable as long as they are 'got to' in time and
given adequate protection and care. However, the sensational approach of the media sometimes backfires on the
agencies. Certain newspapers are prone to stress the
'vice' angle in ways that overshadow and even damage the
case the agencies are trying to present. Centrepoint was
'exposed' for its mixed sleeping arrangements, with heavy
emphasis being placed on the sexual promiscuity of its
clients.

The approach of the media is geared towards getting
'good copy'. Sometimes the attitude is cynical and un-
feeling. When we criticised one reporter for his sensational article about homeless girls becoming striptease
dancers, he replied: 'We're only concerned with selling
newspapers'. An American film director told Centrepoint's director that he would be interested in the
'tragic angle' and the 'juicy bits'. The media fall easy
victims to the exaggerated claims made by some young
people as well as by the agencies. One of our female
subjects admitted to spinning a largely fabricated story
in a televised interview. A natural performer, she had
given her audience what she felt they wanted: a colourful
confirmation of the tragic/at risk stereotype.

Journalists usually came to us with answers rather than
questions and we often felt we were intruding between the
storyline and the notepad. One reporter for instance
asked a string of questions beginning 'Wouldn't you say
that ...?' After thirty minutes of refusing to endorse
her views, she replied: 'You're not being very helpful,
are you?' In her subsequent article, she attributed the
views we did not endorse to 'a social worker'.

Coverage by the media tends to be provoked by illicit
sexuality, drug usage and violence. The case that contained all these ingredients was that of Roger Gleaves in
the TV documentary 'Johnny Go Home'. Gleaves who had
past convictions for sexual offences with young boys set
himself up as director of a voluntary society running
hostels for drifting youngsters. It specialised in
rescuing newcomers on Euston station. Eventually,
Gleaves went back to prison for further sexual offences.
Some of the hostel assistants brutally murdered a young
man called Bill Two Tone, formerly resident in one of the
projects. This case was truly sensational and received
acres of publicity and official reaction. It was completely atypical of the homeless scene: of the stories of
hundreds of young people coming to London each year and
having difficulties in finding accommodation.

The appeal of homelessness lies in the themes of mar-
ginality, loneliness, vulnerability and deprivation.   The
central characters - the homeless and the agency workers -
play out the roles of victims, outsiders or sinners;
champions, befrienders or saviours.   An element of sus-
pense and outrage is provided by a motley collection of
villains: 'property speculators', 'heartless bureau-
crats', 'dirty old men', 'drug pushers', 'pimps', etc.
These dramas have as strong a motif as 'Babes in the
Wood', 'Cinderella', 'Little Red Riding Hood' and Charlie
Chaplin's 'Tramp'.   It is no accident that 'Cathy Come
Home', 'Edna the Inebriate Woman' and 'Johnny Go Home'
have become the fairy tales of our time.

The media's presentation of homelessness is allegori-
cal.   It echoes the converging and confrontation of
opposites - 'Dark and Light'; 'Pauper and Prince'; the
helper and the helpless; the socially responsible and the
wildly impulsive.   There are echoes of Darkest Africa;
the penetration into the underworld; an alien and pagan
jungle peopled by primitives and missionaries.

Such images attract many.   Perhaps the most popular
book on homelessness is Sally Trench's 'Bury me with my
Boots' (Hodder & Stoughton, 1970), which is heavily per-
fumed with Victorian atmosphere, exploration and self-
sacrifice; its author as tragic heroine.   In some respects there are hardly enough people to be rescued.   Most
night shelters have waiting lists of volunteers, posts
advertised with Christian Action (Homeless) often brought
in sixty or seventy applicants, many seeking a drop in
salary.

Work with the homeless may be based on a sense of
humanity, service and inner security or alternatively on
feelings of worthlessness, inadequacy, guilt and oppres-
sion.   In the latter case, it may be a way of acting out
an idealised image of self; of manipulating and dominat-
ing others in the name of 'doing good'; or of vicariously
venting unacknowledged feelings of frustration and self-
pity.

The 'problem' of homelessness is intrinsically bound up
with the self-conceptions and interests of those who
define and respond to it.   Fieldworkers (including volunteers) depend on the homeless for their sense of identity
and/or livelihood.   Even the public sometimes have something at stake.   Largely via the media they derive moral
and economic reference points.   They also obtain emotional stimulation, ranging from pathos to indignation.
For some it may engage the heart; for others it may function as entertainment, voyeurism or as an outlet for un-
discharged emotion.   To a large extent, however, the

feelings and conceptions of the public are being manipula-
ted by the media and the agencies who both have a vested
interest in dramatising and exaggerating the problem.
Some accounts in the media at least, are better regarded
as fairy tales or pornography than as bearing any relation
to the reality.

Chapter 3

THE RESEARCH ARENA:
Participants, settings, perspectives and methods

This chapter looks at those involved in the research and
the relationships, contexts and considerations that affected its conduct and outcome.   We do not regard ourselves
as neutral observers, somehow aloof and detached from the
drama we describe.   Nor were we seen as such.   What we
observed of the agencies or our subjects depended on our
relationships with them.   These were not formed in isolation.   We became incorporated in a network of interdepen-
dent, emotionally charged relationships inside which we
could not usually preserve a separate identity as 'independent researchers'.   Subjects tended to see us as ex-
tensions of the agencies or 'officialdom';   the agencies,
as appendages of our sponsors or the media (although they
still demanded that our primary allegiance should go to
them).

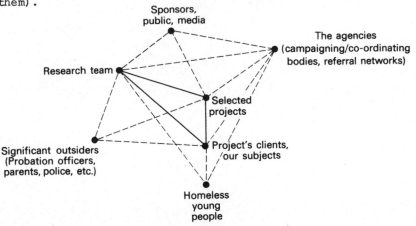

FIGURE 3.1   The research arena

The agencies and ourselves shared a similar public or

audience, which included our sponsors, the DHSS.   Many
voluntary agencies were anxious about our linking them to
the public or government in ways that might threaten their
interests.   One major fear was that we might depict their
clients as 'deviants' rather than 'victims' and so undermine popular support.   We were often seen as renegades or
mavericks and as such untrustworthy and irresponsible.
Centrepoint expressed the anxiety that we might be 'spies
of the DHSS'.   On the other hand, WERC and North responded positively to us, partly because they felt they had
more to gain than lose from exposure.

These attitudes towards us - often guarded and sometimes overtly hostile - inevitably coloured our views of
the agencies.   They also affected the amount of co-operation we received.   Centrepoint, for instance, tried to
control and limit our access to its clients.   It even
halted our sampling programme for several months until
some of its anxieties had been resolved.   These partly
arose out of its concern to protect clients from intrusion, intimidation and breaches of confidentiality.   However, Centrepoint was also concerned about our challenging
its presentation of the 'problem' and so undermining its
credibility and the effectiveness of its campaigning
effort.   On this score, its anxiety was reinforced by
other agencies with which it was collaborating.   Centrepoint's response placed us in an analogous position to its
clients: we too had to qualify for admission by showing
ourselves to be bona fide deserving cases.

Our subjects were selected for interview under the
auspices of one or other of the three selected projects.
The context of the project was important in two ways.

First, it variously affected whom we were likely to
select for interview and thus the representiveness of the
sample.   The likelihood of a prospective subject being
selected depended on his reaching the project, being
granted admission and his length of stay.   These in turn
depended on the project's policy, accessibility and referral networks and on the preferences and alternative
options of the client.

Second, the context of the project was likely to affect
what our subjects told us and thus the validity of the
data.   Despite our protestations that we were independent
research workers and that information given would be kept
confidential, subjects often tended to identify us with
the project.   This caused them to limit, slant or counterfeit the information given, either to guard against the
possibility of us informing on them or in the hope that we
might exert a positive influence on their behalf.   For
instance, subjects having mis-represented themselves as

under twenty-five to gain admission to Centrepoint were
likely to stick to the inaccuracy in their interviews with
us.   The extent to which the workers at each project
trusted, welcomed or identified with us may have subtly
affected the ways subjects perceived and responded to us.
Our reception at North and WERC was warm, at Centrepoint
cool or hostile.   However, we were closer in outlook,
background and appearance to Centrepoint workers than to
those at North and far removed from those at WERC.

Other relationships also intruded into our interactions
with subjects.   Quite a few had reason to keep their
whereabouts hidden from police, parents or probation
officers.   This often led them to disguise their identity
and origins in case we or the projects informed on them.
A few subjects even saw us as linking them to the 'powers
that be' or to an audience they might play to.

Our research also took place in other contexts, somewhat removed from the homeless scene.   There was the
'backroom' aspect of our research, performed with an eye
to the expectations of our professional peer groups in the
more general fields of research and social work.   There
was also the process of following up subjects one year
later (which we look at in chapter 8).

ELICITING AND CHECKING OUR SUBJECT'S STORIES (AND THE
EXTENT AND NATURE OF FALSE INFORMATION)

The initial tape recorded interview of an hour or more was
our main access to the worlds from which our subjects
came.   This access was broadened, wherever possible, by
the follow-up interview and by communication with relatives, friends, probation officers and social workers in
the course of relocating them or checking their stories.

The interview was flexibly structured with few standardised questions.   We aimed at an informal, free-ranging
overtly empathetic approach.   In this way, we hoped to
promote rapport and trust.   As an incentive to take part,
subjects were paid a £1 fee.

The subjects seemed to define us in various ways.   We
were sometimes identified with the project workers as, for
instance, 'social workers' or 'officials' and responded to
either as potential sources of advice, support and attention or as someone officially 'asking questions'.   As the
latter, we might be seen as someone to help, indulge, ward
off or tease.   They might, for instance, make us the butt
of tall stories.   Alternatively, subjects sometimes saw
us as quite independent of the project (and even of 'officialdom' in general) - to the extent of revealing informa-

tion that they had concealed from project workers.   This
was especially so in the case of WERC.

These comments illustrate various ways in which we
might have been seen:

'I trust social workers and I tell you more than I
would them.'
'It's good to have a chance to get things off your
chest.'
'I've told you things I wouldn't tell my girlfriend.'
'It [what I tell you] might help someone else.'
'I would talk to you normally if you weren't doing a
survey.'
'I don't know what this survey's about ... I don't
trust anybody.'

Often we achieved a rapport with our subjects that
bridged the gap between our differing positions.   Caroline was more successful at this than Euan or Kim.   Far
fewer of her subjects gave false names and/or addresses.
Females especially seemed more relaxed and open with her.
For instance, 'I can say things to you I couldn't to a
bloke.'   Another female later wrote, 'Thank you, you
really helped me sort out my problems.   You've really
been a good friend to me.'   Males were more inclined to
impress her with their daring exploits or survival expertise.

We received a substantial quantity of false information.   At first we lamented this but later gave value to
it as an inevitable part not only of our research but of
the whole homelessness process.   The agencies constantly
encountered this problem.   We, however, had more time and
resources to probe and check subjects' stories.

We have routinely checked their parents' or relatives'
names and addresses through electoral registers.   Where
possible (with their permission) we checked their accounts
with probation officers or social workers, with project
records and occasionally with parents, workplaces or
school.   We have referred to official records on births,
marriages and deaths.

We tended to cross-examine subjects fairly intensively
and pin down details.   On playing back tapes we listened
for inconsistencies and other indications that they might
be lying.   For instance, where subjects left periods unaccounted for, it might be because they were concealing
time spent in an institution or, in the case of subjects
around fifteen and sixteen years, were overstating their
ages.

Several interviewees were incompetent liars.   Two

males giving false names let their real ones slip out.
'Well Brian, he said - I mean David ...'.   A girl
forgot the month she was recently 'married' in.   Two
other girls gave dates of birth that did not coincide with
their stated ages.

However, inconsistencies did not necessarily imply that
a subject was lying.   Some subjects seemed genuinely confused about dates and sequences in their lives.   For example, when re-interviewed, one girl sincerely thought she
had been in London for two to three months whereas we were
able to establish that she had been there only two weeks
(before being arrested for jumping bail).

For most of the sample it has been possible to check
only a small part of the account given.   We had to make
judgments about veracity but with the checks made, we discovered a high degree of correlation between our judgment
and the facts.   However, in two cases the implausible
turned out to be true.   One girl's mother was murdered by
a rebuffed lover and one youth's brother was deaf and dumb
and a factory manager.

Our subjects have been classified in the tables in this
book according to information given unless this has been
contradicted or supplemented by a reliable source or
unless slips and inconsistencies strongly indicate inaccu-
racies.   In the few cases where we are certain that a
respondent has given false information and we do not know
the correct information, we have placed them in the false/
unreliable data category.

Despite our sceptical approach, some data presented is
likely to be invalid.   One can anticipate the likely bias
away from the truth.   Our experience has born out that
subjects in most cases tend to understate the extent of
deviant activities, interpersonal difficulties and uncom-
fortable feelings such as anxiety, inadequacy and despera-
tion;   and tend to overstate motivations or performance in
areas like education and work.

One index of veracity is the number giving false names
and/or addresses.   We asked subjects to give an address
through which we could contact them for re-interview.
The table below shows the numbers giving false recontact
addresses and/or names, or who gave no address.

The correctness of names and addresses was established
through various checks involving the electoral register,
birth records and social services.   Altogether twenty
males and nine females gave false addresses;   of these,
five males and one female gave real names.   A further ten
males and two females would or could not give a recontact
address, but at least eight of these gave a real name.   A
further three males gave a false name but real address.

TABLE 3.1 Numbers giving false addresses and/or false names or no recontact addresses

	Male	Female
False address and possibly or probably false name	15	8
False address but real name	5	1
False name but real address	3	-
Claims to have no recontact address but gives real name	4	1
Claims to have no recontact address and possible false name	3	-
Refused to give address but gave real name	3	-
Refused to give address and possible false name	-	1
Total (of individuals listed)	33	11

As far as we could establish, the remaining thirty-nine males and twenty-four famales in our sample gave correct names and addresses.

False information did not always prevent us from checking stories or relocating them in the follow up. Of those giving false names and/or addresses, three males and one female gave the actual name of their probation officer or social worker, as did two males claiming they had no address to give.

Where subjects gave us false addresses or none at all, we tended to suspect they were concealing something significant such as being 'on the run' or 'running away from home'. For instance, two young males who gave conflict with parents as their reason for coming to London were - as we later discovered - absconding from community homes. In a further interview, one told us: 'I gave you slightly false information in case I was tracked - I thought you was a government officer'. Two girls gave false names and addresses fearing that they might be returned home because they were 'under age'.

However, failure to give a correct name and/or address did not necessarily imply that a subject's account was unreliable. One male refused to give an address because of the shame if his parents found out he was homeless and another because he did not want 'someone coming round and checking up on me' or 'forms coming through the door'. The latter compared us with the police - 'once they get your name and address they never stop: they tell you to

do this and that'.   The strategy of giving a false
address might even allow a subject to be more honest, as
seemed the case with two males who admitted being 'on the
run' from the law.

Several stories were later found to be substantially
false.   Some were lying for purely instrumental reasons.
They wanted to conceal that they were on the run or to
keep their story consistent with false information ensur-
ing admission to the selected project.   Some wished to
conceal information of which they were ashamed.   One male
only revealed that he had twice been in prison just before
the end of the interview.   'You don't expect me to tell
people I've been in jail ... it would make me look silly
[and] feel ashamed of myself.'   Whilst others wanted to
gain our sympathy or interest by projecting some new
image.

Five females were implausibly melodramatic and recounted the sudden deaths of loved ones.   We describe them as
the 'tragic heroines'.   For example, one, aged sixteen,
told of the death of her successful father and beautiful
mother in the Munich air disaster.   This left her an
heiress to a legacy controlled by a crippled guardian.
'All they could find of my mother was her arm and her hand
still with this ring on it.   I wear it all the time.   I
never take it off.'   She actually had been living with
real parents just before coming to London.   In her story,
they became wicked foster-parents.   They fostered her to
make money.   Her 'foster-father' attacked her leading to
court cases and hospitalisation, while her 'foster-mother'
beat her over the head with a Christmas tree.   She was
raped at six years old by a West Indian, leaving her
frigid.   She lost a boyfriend in a motorcycle crash -
'everyone I ever loved gets killed'.   She invented a fictitious step-sister, the same age as herself who was
'naughty and dirty'.

Another, aged twenty-one told of six deaths happening
to friends and relatives, including her fiancé to which
she responded by dramatic suicide attempts described in
detail.   'I did it [attempted suicide] to punish myself
because I couldn't get what I wanted - someone to get
close to who wouldn't hurt me ... everybody I've been
close to gets killed ... death has blighted my life'.

A further girl aged sixteen claimed she had been the
cause of her boyfriend's death.   He jumped from a balcony
in a crowded dance hall.   She spent three days at his
bedside.   'He said he loved me and that I was not to
blame myself.   I know I'll be with him again one day.'
She also had a brother who died in a motorcycle crash, and
invented a twin brother who was very close to her.   She

claimed that her mother put the children away in a home
because 'she was too poor to feed us'.

Of the remaining two 'tragic heroines', one, who was in
fact illegitimate, claimed that her father was destroyed
in a 'brick-smashing machine', and the other that her
father and her boyfriend were both killed in motorcycle
crashes - the latter just after she had become pregnant.

Three males recounted fictitious death stories.   The
father of one and the non-existent twin brother of another
were both 'shot' while serving in Northern Ireland.   The
other had recently 'lost' his parents in a car crash.

These stories seemed a way of commanding our attention.
The five women especially were aspiring actresses (and
playwrights), using the interview as a stage instead of
conveying prosaic details.   One said, 'I want to write a
play, but I want to star in it ... I like the limelight'.
Another asked, 'Are we going to be on TV?'   At a metaphorical level, they were perhaps being unusually open.
They were sharing themselves emotionally if not accurate-
ly.   They wanted us to feel along with them; to become
absorbed in their drama.   They were using their accounts
poetically as a vehicle to demonstrate their capacities
for love, strong feeling and profound experience.   Perhaps their fantasies were the main and only outlet for
feelings of love and intimacy.   By 'killing off' loved
ones, they could reside in an idealised world and indulge
feelings of sadness, grief and feeling unloved.

A few subjects assumed a completely different identity.
The most extreme case was that of a male, aged twenty-one,
selected at WERC.   The interviewer (Kim) was non-plussed
by his reticence until some other clients explained he was
deaf and dumb.   From his written replies, we learned he
was dumb but not deaf.   His parents had recently been
killed in an M1 car crash.   This had prompted him to
leave Yorkshire to seek out his only living relative.
However, on his first day in London he discovered that the
relative had emigrated; he also lost his wallet containing £60.   Two weeks later, Kim came across him again at
Centrepoint.   As if by some miracle, he had become a vol-
uble Scotsman.   This time the lost wallet contained £187
and he had come to London because of 'boredom.   I was in
a rut.'   He brazened it out: 'I can see the baffled look
on your face but I've no seen you before....   Dumb?   I
couldn't see me being dumb.   If I sat there for more than
ten minutes I'd burst out with a mouthful.'   His hand-
writing and appearance were unmistakably the same, and he
gave the same date of birth (although different names) on
both occasions.

This young man had fooled WERC for three weeks - the

resettlement officer had noted 'deaf and dumb but a good
lip reader'.   This extravagant pretence could well have
been a way of turning the tables on those in positions of
power and expertise, motivated by the desire to be top dog
in an underdog situation.   By getting the social worker,
official or researcher to fall for a tall story, the
client or respondent can invert the power and status dif-
ferential: the 'expert' is shown to be a fool; the
'puller of strings' is reduced to a puppet; the sympathi-
ser is made out to be pathetic; and the labeller is himself labelled (as a dupe and possibly as a mental defective).   The interaction resembles a contest between an
angler and a wily fish (in which the fish catches the
angler).   The inquisitor/helper tries to hook the respon-
dent/client with questions and encapsulate him inside a
net of categories.   Instead he is himself 'hooked', be-
guiled by the answers he receives.   The fish not only
gets away but also has the satisfaction of watching the
angler trying to land a large empty can and toppling into
the water in the process.

However, only a few of our subjects' accounts can be
seen as essentially false as opposed to essentially true.
The subjects were engaged in the same process as we and
the agencies were - that of presenting themselves with a
view to securing resources, sympathy and attention and
safeguarding their interests.   The homeless young people
are at the base of a hierarchy of self-justification.
The agencies are continually presenting a case for funding
and public support, sometimes exaggerating considerably
the size of the 'problem'.   Sponsoring bodies such as the
Government have to justify their handling of the 'problem'
- to the media and through them to the public.

RELATING TO THE AGENCIES

The agencies and workers were a backcloth against which we
studied our subjects.   The workers often questioned and
interrogated us about the nature of our research and we
felt more like subjects, even defendants, than researchers.   By calling ourselves 'researchers' and being the
recipients of a DHSS grant, we were a focus of concern and
anxiety.

Many agencies felt the research was a waste of money as
everything useful was known about the homeless.   The research money should have been used to provide increased
facilities.   It was obviously a device to avoid action.
Resentment was strongest among those emphasising the political aspects of homelessness.   They suspected we had

received the grant because we would individuate the
problem thereby excusing the government from action.
The catch went like this:

If you find that individual choices predominate in
homelessness this will confirm the irrelevant and
basically capitalistic nature of your research.   If
you confirm that economic factors are most important
you prove that the research was a waste of money.

Our original research postulates, emerging from a one-
year pilot study, were given to Centrepoint and then
leaked to other agencies.   These postulates confirmed
their worst anxieties.   In particular, one went: 'the
sample would show a very high incidence of "deviant" behaviour and social processing before their arrival in
London.'   This confirmed the 'individuation' fears and in
their view threatened to alienate public sympathy.
Vainly we explained that our postulates represented questions rather than conclusions.
   In the preliminary stages of our work, a few voluntary
agencies (including the Soho Project, CHAR, New Horizon,
and After Six) were mounting a vehement attack on the prevailing 'pathological' model in favour of a 'political'
one.   Some of that attack was focused on us, even though
we had serious doubts about the 'pathological' model.
   In January 1974 we heard informally of a document in
circulation listing criticisms about our research.   This
document had never been discussed with, or sent to, us.
We suggested a meeting with the agencies.
   The meeting was crowded out and waxed passionate for
several hours.   Arguments ranged from simple abuse to a
confusion about the terms 'postulate' and 'conclusion'.
The meeting seemed to do little to resolve deep differences despite the fact that we had, and still have, much
respect for most agencies involved in homelessness.
   Whereas workers in statutory agencies were often pre-
occupied with career prospects, the voluntary agency workers had a strong sense of responsibility towards their
clients.   They took on the mantle of guardian or 'friend
of the friendless'.   Often this sense of responsibility
seemed related to vicarious guilt as the clients were perceived as victims of a harsh society.   They tried to live
up to exceptionally high standards.   Their aspirations
for clients far exceeded what could be achieved realisti-
cally.   The inevitable sense of disappointment influenced
their pessimistic picture of the problem.
   They invested much in the homeless.   We seemed to be
undermining their commitment, threatening to challenge

their ideological models.   Privately, the clients themselves presented considerable sources of frustration.   A
large number did not 'seem motivated to help themselves'.
Clients seemed to postpone decisions and efforts that
might ensure the less immediate future in favour of living
in the 'here and now' and focusing on present problems and
needs.   This frustrated the 'helping' process.

Workers also face internal resistances.   In struggling
to live up to some idealised image they might fight tendencies not to care, to vent exasperations on clients and
to be 'self-indulgent'.   Many young recruits last only a
few months to a year before exhaustion and disenchantment
overcome them.   Among the few who last longer, the strain
can be a form of self-flagellation.   In the homeless
field, 'breakdowns' tend to be an occupational hazard.

The agencies often lacked continuity and were constantly being thrown back on a circle of problems met almost
annually.   They were always adjusting to new intakes of
staff.   Workers were recruited for a sense of mission and
political or religious commitment.   Idealism was preferred to pragmatism.   There was suspicion of the more
structured and less impassioned approach of the professional.

Although it was implied in campaigning documents and
reports that organisations were overloaded with clients,
this was not always the case.   Numbers fluctuated greatly
in most projects.   Many suffered from a shortage of
clients for much of each year.   They went to great pains
to explain this - it was due to increased police activity,
IRA bombing, the hot weather, the Christmas period.   When
numbers rose, it was claimed that the long awaited inva-
sion was here: unemployment and the contraction in the
accommodation market were finally biting.

They had an investment in the growth of the problem.
They need homeless young people to support the viability
of their projects.   Quantity was something the public and
government understood.   How many?   How many?   Even more
importantly, homeless people were needed to justify a view
of the nature of society.   They were needed as victims of
a cruel and uncaring community.

SELECTING THE SAMPLE AND RELATING IT TO A POPULATION

Sampling procedures and selection criteria

Usually in research, the target population is defined and
a selection process devised.   This involves constructing
a 'sampling frame' - a list of all members of the target

population, including knowledge of where individuals may
be contacted.   This allows for random sampling, generally
the most reliable means of representing a population.

This process is impossible with homeless young people,
given our baseline definition of homelessness, ie those
currently using emergency accommodation, eg reception
centres, night shelters, crash pads, all-night cafés,
clubs and cinemas, sleeping on floors, sleeping rough,
derelict houses, short stay hostels, lodging houses,
squats and cheap hotels or bed and breakfast.   This population is constantly shifting as individuals enter and
leave the London homeless scene.   People are continually
moving from one project, squat and crash pad to another.
It is impossible to know the entire population or even to
have a rough idea of size or of distribution between various settings.

Daunted by these complications, we approached the problem from the other end.   First, we constructed a viable
method of selection and then dealt with what population
this selected sample might represent.   For reasons of
feasibility, our sample came entirely from the three agencies already described.   These three projects provided a
large slice of the emergency residential provision for
homeless young people new to London, at the time of our
research.   Their styles and client types also reflected
diversity in provision.   The main sources of our sample,
Centrepoint and WERC, had a comparatively large turnover
of clients and were close to our Soho base.   'North', a
smaller project, expanded our sample of provision.   It
was based outside central London at Highgate and tended to
resemble crash pad accommodation.

The sample was restricted to users of selected projects
who were under twenty-six years old, had arrived in London
within the last two months and who were either completely
new to the GLC area, or, prior to their present stay, had
experienced a near-continuous absence from London dating
back to a minimum of one year before the date of the
interview.   By this last condition we meant that, in the
period beginning one year ago and ending two months before
the time of the interview, they must have experienced no
more than three stays in London and no one continuous stay
of more than two weeks.

This definition included those 'new' to London in the
sense of returning after a longish gap as well as those
visiting briefly in the last year.   Many people visit
London for holidays, football matches or pop concerts.
Excluding these people from our sample might have involved
bias in favour of those living long distances from London.

Sampling spanned a thirteen-month period from April

1974 to May 1975.   The sampling avoided selection bias by
interviewers.   Project users were 'screened' against our
selection criteria and we selected the first 'eligible'
individual agreeing to be interviewed.

Separate quotas of males and females were selected at
the two mixed projects, Centrepoint and North.   Five men
and a pair of girls refused to be screened or interviewed.
Seven people, all males, were excluded from our sample
because we discovered either during the interview or in
later checking, that they were ineligible.

Sample characteristics

TABLE 3.2 Sample: by project and sex

Project	Males	Females	Total
Centrepoint	29	29	58
WERC	34	–	34
North	9	6	15
Total	72	35	107

Table 3.2 gives our sample size and the breakdown by
project and sex.   Of the seventy-two males and thirty-
five females selected and initially interviewed, we
managed to follow up and re-interview twenty-nine males
(40 per cent) and sixteen females (46 per cent).

We now look at the way our sample is distributed in
terms of our selection criteria: age and time in London.

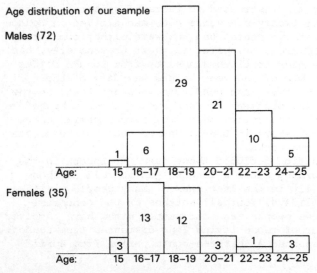

FIGURE 3.2 Age distribution of sample

TABLE 3.3 Average ages – by project

Project	Male	Female
Centrepoint	20.1	19.0
WERC	21.6	–
North	20.4	20.7
All projects	20.8	19.3

About 70 per cent of males were aged between eighteen and twenty-one (inclusive), 72 per cent of the females were aged between sixteen and nineteen years of age. Seven males, all from Centrepoint, were seventeen or under: sixteen girls, all but two from Centrepoint, were aged seventeen or under. Centrepoint men were on average 1½ years younger than men from WERC; the average age for all females is about 1½ years less than for all the men. There was a tendency for younger subjects to overstate their actual age and for older persons to understate them.

Three Centrepoint girls posing as seventeen either admitted during the course of the interview or we discovered later were one or two years younger. One North girl, pretending to be sixteen, eventually confided that she was fifteen – 'Don't tell anyone, will you? I don't want to be sent back home.' Two Centrepoint males posing as nineteen and seventeen were later found to be sixteen and fifteen respectively.

We strongly suspect that two girls claiming to be eighteen and seventeen from Centrepoint were overstating their ages, but their claimed ages are in the table. Two Centrepoint males and one from North falsely gave their ages as under twenty-six and were subsequently excluded from the sample. One Centrepoint female claiming to be nineteen was actually twenty-four but still within our target population.

TABLE 3.4 Previously in London

	Male	Female
Within last two years only	13	7
Two years or more ago only	17	8
In both the above periods	6	2
Never before	36	18
Total	72	35

Table 3.4 shows the number visiting London prior to

their present stay.   Half of the male sample and just over half (51.5 per cent) of the females claimed never to have been in London before this present visit.

Table 3.5 shows that 57 per cent of men and 63 per cent of women were, when interviewed, within the first week of their present stay in London.   Thirty-nine per cent of males and 51.5 per cent of females had only been in London for two complete nights or less at the time of the initial interview.

TABLE 3.5   Length of time in London before the interview (current stay only)

	Male	Female
Two complete nights or less	28	18
Up to one week	13	4
One week to two weeks	15	6
Two weeks to one month	9	2
One month to two months	5	5
False/unreliable data	2	-
Total	72	35

Relating our sample to a population

What population does our sample represent?   In no way does it represent the wider population of homeless young newcomers to London since it excludes those using other agencies or simply not using any.   We might expect significant differences between our sample and people surviving without formal help.   The latter might be more resourceful or provident or perhaps more amenable to sleeping rough.   The boyfriend of one subject, homeless for many months, still refused to use agencies because of possible 'third degree' treatment.

At best, the sample represents that population of homeless young people who, whilst still relatively new to London, stay in the three selected projects.   Even in this respect the sample is liable to be severely biased since the probability of any eligible project user being selected was proportional to his length of stay.   Bias may arise from two sources: project policy and consumer choice.   The length of stay may be dependent on decisions made by project workers.   Some users tend to be classed as more 'deserving' or 'needy' than others and thus allowed to stay longer.   Bias on this score is more

likely to be significant at Centrepoint.   Consumer choice
is more likely to lead to bias in the case of WERC and
North where time limits were less fixed and users were
usually allowed to stay much longer.   Centrepoint users
were usually told they would not be re-admitted after
staying from between one to four nights.   WERC did ask a
small minority to leave - for instance, those who do not
appear to be seriously looking for work - but this did not
usually occur until at least the second week of stay.

What direction might this bias take?   There might be
significant differences in lifestyle and background between those who found the formality and paternalism of
WERC acceptable and those who did not.   The former, tend-
ing to stay longer, were more likely to be selected.   At
North, those attracted to 'alternative' lifestyles might
tend to stay longer.   At all three projects, those who
were more resourceful or reluctant to be in a dependent
position might leave earlier.

Centrepoint favoured those perceived to be 'at risk'
and 'motivated' to find work and accommodation in London.
Those at the bottom end of the age-spectrum tended to be
seen as more vulnerable and thus allowed to stay longer.
This bias was evident in our sample.   The median ages of
our Centrepoint male and female sample quotas were both
one year less than the median ages for the total number of
males and females (under twenty-five) using Centrepoint in
1975.   Admission and re-admission depended on self-pre-
sentation as well as selection criteria.   For example,
one subject would have been admitted to Centrepoint the
first time he applied if he had not told the worker at the
gate that he was only planning to pass through London.
Persistence might be rewarded as with one female subject
who kept ringing Centrepoint's bell until the exasperated
worker eventually let her stay.   As the worker said:
'What can you do?'   Workers might vary in the way they
applied formal criteria.   For instance, to justify referring a young man on to WERC, one Centrepoint worker laid
stress on his being an ex-serviceman.   This, she felt,
implied resilience and resourcefulness. (1)

A client's choice as to whether to seek help, how to
present his request, how to make use of help if it is
offered, is guided by norms which the social worker may
not know about and may not share.   The social worker
has perspectives and acts on cues which are not visible
to the client and which the social worker may not even
make explicit.

The possible extent of bias can be gauged from a com-

parison between the average length of stay for all project
users and the average for the sample.   Follow-up members
of our WERC quota stayed for an average of 10.3 days compared with an average of only 2.5 days for all users.
Follow-up males and females in our Centrepoint quota
stayed an average of 3.1 and 4.1 days respectively compared with an average of 1.9 and 2.1 for all users.

TABLE 3.6   Estimated total number of different individuals
under twenty-six years old using each project over a one-
year period and eligible for inclusion in our sample
(1974-5)

Project			Eligible proportions	
			Males	Females
Centrepoint			1060	494
WERC			1375	-
North			162	110
Totals	(a)	Summed populations	2597	604
	(b)	Combined populations (corrected for individuals using more than one project)	2172	586

   We have calculated rough estimates of the size of project populations from which our sample was drawn.   Our
population figures are based on figures provided by the
different projects: for North over a nine-month period
in 1974-5;   for Centrepoint for a twelve-month period
during 1975;   for WERC for a two-month period during the
summer of 1975, two months after our sampling had
finished.
   Information from the projects does not include details
about 'newness' to London but from our 'screening' opera-
tion we calculate the approximate proportion of users eligible for selection.   We found that of all individuals
under twenty-six screened at each project, respectively
57 per cent, 42 per cent and 75 per cent of males at
Centrepoint, WERC and North were eligible and 74 per cent
and 83 per cent of females at Centrepoint and North were
eligible.
   The total population of different individuals using the
three selected projects would be less than the sum of the
project populations.   What is the overlap in usage?
Centrepoint records showed that 24 per cent of our WERC

sample, 33 per cent of our North male sample and 17 per cent of our North female sample stayed there during their first two months in London.   These figures are unreliable for the North sub-sample because of the tiny figures and further complicated by the tendency to use false names.

We estimate that about a quarter of the WERC population would already have been counted as part of the male Centrepoint population.   Allowing for this and also for those double-counted and possibly treble-counted for North, we estimate that the adjusted combined male population is 2172 and the combined female population at 586.

We present our sample findings separately for males and females, since the combined sample over-represents the latter.   However, in the case of either sex, we lump together the sample quotas taken from each project.   This was done for the sake of simplicity and to ensure a sample size (for either sex) that was large enough to support reasonable generalisations.

Females constituted a minority within the populations of the selected projects so we deliberately over-represented them to ensure an adequate sample size.   The ratio of males to females at Centrepoint was 2.1:1 whereas in our sample it is 1:1.   The ratio of males to females at North was almost the same for both population and sample (1.48:1 and 1.5:1).

Since in the case of either sex, we generalise on the basis of the combined sample, it is important that sample quotas are proportional to their respective populations. If we assume that our estimates for the projects' populations are correct then the figures for either sex taken separately compare well.   Table 3.7 compares the male sample quotas at each project with their relative population sizes.   Figures in brackets next to the sample and population percentages respectively show the numbers selected at each project and the numbers we should have selected to achieve proportional representation of the summed population of the three projects.

TABLE 3.7 Degree of proportionality between sample quotas for projects and their actual population sizes (males only)

	Sample proportion	Proportion of summed population of all three projects
Centrepoint	40.5% (29)	41% (29.5)
WERC	47% (34)	53% (38)
North	12.5% (9)	6% (4.5)
Total	100% (72)	100% (72)

As Table 3.7 shows, our combined male sample marginally under-represents the reception centre population and considerably over-represents that of North.   The proportion of Centrepoint males in our sample and in our estimate   of the summed population is similar.   Over-representation of North males was intentional because we wished to select enough individuals to generalise about this project.   The ratio of Centrepoint females to North females in the sample is similar to the ratio of the populations: in the sample 4.8:1 and for the population 4.5:1.

In combining the sample quotas from each project we are by implication amalgamating their populations.   This is a rather questionable expedient given that our choice of projects for sampling was somewhat arbitrary.   In addition, the minority who use more than one of the selected projects tend to make themselves more available for selection and thus are liable to be over-represented in our combined sample.   These individuals may actually be different from those who only use one project.   For instance, they may stay longer on the homeless scene.   They may be more resourceful in exploiting this segment of the provision or alternatively they may be less able or less inclined to survive outside of it.   However, this is only one aspect of a more general failing in our sampling scheme: the longer a newcomer to London uses (or is allowed to use) one or more of the three selected projects, the greater the probability of this person appearing in our sample.

OUR APPROACH TO THE RESEARCH

Here we look at some of the considerations that shaped our research methods and perspectives.

We were rather ambivalent about using orthodox research procedures.   We wanted to conduct our research in a 'professional' manner, but increasingly had severe doubts about the validity and feasibility of such notions as 'reliable', 'objective' and 'representative'.   We did attempt to apply orthodox sampling procedures.   However, even if we had obtained a 'representative' sample, the context of our interviews was far from being representative of the other life contexts of the subjects to which we wished to generalise.   Nor were we a 'representative' sample of observers.   The whole notion is questionable as one reporter found out when he asked a demonstrating student whom he represented.   The reply: 'I am a group of individuals.'

In our approach to the interviewing, we departed from

orthodox assumptions and practices.   Instead of standar-
dising the order and wording of the questions and adopting
the role of the impersonal, detached, 'standardised' researcher, we aimed at a style that was 'chatty', flexible,
open-ended and personally involved.   Rather than confin-
ing the subjects to our dimensions, we gave them scope to
provide their own.   Instead of simply taking our subjects' words at face value, we sought to probe beneath
appearances and use our capacity for empathy and intuition.

   The notion of 'reliable' data assumes the possibility
of removing the personal or subjective element from the
research process.   In the social scientist's lexicon
observations are 'reliable', when made according to specified procedures and standardised conditions so that they
could be replicated, in principle at least, by others con-
forming to those specifications.   However, although it is
possible to standardise the wording of questions, it is
impossible to standardise their meaning or the contexts
in which they are asked.   Even if it were possible to
standardise the role of the observer, this may be counterproductive.   For instance, the veracity of subjects'
accounts hinged on our perceived trustworthiness.   By
opening ourselves up we felt able to melt some initial
distrust.   Our data might not be obtained by other 'observers' but paradoxically may have greater validity precisely because the observing role was not standardised.

   Our style of interviewing turned out to have several
advantages over the standardised questionnaire.   It encouraged many of our subjects to gradually open themselves
up and allowed us to approach each area from varying
angles, some of which might be more fruitful than others.
As we learned, subjects' earlier replies and especially
those in response to direct questions - for instance, 'why
did you come to London?' - were often misleading as was
clear from remarks later in the interview.   Sometimes
subjects were unforthcoming in response to direct questioning, finding our dimensions unfamiliar, irrelevant or
confusing or this approach presumptuous and intrusive.
They preferred to tell us in their own way and time.
The length and relatively open-ended nature of the interview allowed scope for the subject to reveal more sides or
let slip something he was trying to hide.   For instance,
it took one subject $1\frac{1}{2}$ hours before he confessed to jumping bail.

   However, this approach - partly because it was so successful - presented severe headaches in the coding and
analysis stages.   Since we were applying a case-study
approach to a relatively large sample, we were faced with

too much information.   Our approach allowed us to see
that subjects' accounts were often inconsistent or implausible.   They had scope to contradict themselves and
we had space to test the validity of their initial
replies.   Subjects might for instance, be in conflict or
uncertain about their motivations or be unable to reliably
recall the dates and details of past events.   There was
always the question of whether a subject was being honest
or trying to mislead us.   Should we code his remarks on
the basis of what he told us or should we give more weight
to what we sensed was 'really' the case?   At what point
did we decide that our credulity was being stretched too
far?

Such difficulties in interpreting and summarising the
raw data could often only be resolved by relying on an
overa-all impression.   The recourse to impressionistic
judgment created in us a sense of insecurity.   We craved
the security of hard data - for instance, a concrete
remark to a specific question - on which to base our
judgments.   However, we were comforted by the realisation
that a subject's reply could only be safely interpreted in
the light of the total picture we had built up of him and
especially his perception of the interview context.

We increasingly came to value our subjectivity - the
bane of the orthodox researcher.   We reacted against the
'value-free, value-neutral and value-avoiding model of
science', which leads researchers to believe they can
somehow stand outside the events being studied. (2)   In
contrast, we saw ourselves as an integral part of them.
Given the hostile responses of some agency workers, we
soon abandoned any illusion that we could be detached or
aloof.   When we observed subjects or the agencies, we
were as much on stage as in the audience.   The picture we
present bears the stamp of our intervention.   It is also
partly our projection.   It reflects our social position
and incorporates the values, preconceptions and life experiences against which we 'measured' those of others.

So we drifted away from orthodox scientific method and
learned to respect our intuition and experience.   As
Phillips comments: '[if sociologists are] really concerned with the meaning of social action, then the actor
and his actions cannot be viewed wholly from the perspective of the outside, detached observer.' (3)   We sought
after meaning not only in the external sense but also in-
ternally.   'Often what we know best, most deeply and
truly, is what we have directly experienced ourselves.
We often understand what a certain phenomenon "means" because we, ourselves, have experienced it.' (4)

Homelessness is an important reference point for us.

David was homeless in London at the age of fifteen which
motivated a longstanding involvement, both as an agency
worker and commentator.   Kim lived under the threat of
eviction for many months and was actually homeless for a
few days after being illegally evicted - headlined as 'The
Menace of the Masked Landlady' by the 'News of the World'!
    This process of identification, common among the more
radical agency workers could of course be taken too far.
We were all far removed from the social situation of our
subjects.   Some came from seemingly alien cultures.   Two
subjects bore numerous stab and slash marks to testify to
involvement in the Glasgow street gangs.
    We tend to give the misleading impression that the re-
search team is a homogenous entity.   However, there were
often disagreements between us.   One of these, for instance, concerned the weight attached to macro-economic
factors in generating and sustaining homelessness.   David
and Kim took for granted structural factors which had been
extensively researched and were more interested in the
homeless as individuals.   Caroline and Ewan, who joined
the research team later, stressed the political implications of our report.   They felt we could unintentionally
provide fodder for those preferring to see homeless young
people simply as inadequates or deviants rather than working towards the removal of economic root causes.

Chapter 4

DIFFERING PERSPECTIVES

This chapter looks at the ways our subjects viewed their situation and compares these with the perspectives of the agencies.

'HOMELESS?'

We rarely heard our subjects use 'homeless'. If they explicitly defined the situation at all, they used terms
like 'nowhere to kip', 'no money', 'down', 'looking for a
flat and job', 'seeking experience/adventure/anonymity' or
hiding out from the police or parents.
    We asked a large portion of our subjects if they saw
themselves as homeless.

TABLE 4.1 Responses to the question 'Do you see yourself
as homeless?'

	Males	Females
Yes	45	22
No	16	9
Ambivalent	3	-
Don't know	2	-
Question not asked	6	4
Total	72	35

TABLE 4.2 Main factor in deciding whether or not
'homeless'

	Males			Females		
	Yes	No	Ambivalent	Yes	No	Ambivalent
Emotional relationships	7	-	-	1	-	-
(Un)employment	-	1	-	-	1	-
Accommodation (or lack of) outside London	2	10	2	4	3	-
Accommodation (or lack of) in London	37	5	-	17	5	-
Total	46	16	2	22	9	-

In the vast majority of cases our subjects defined
homelessness primarily in material terms rather than emotional ones.   There were eight exceptions (seven males).
These felt homeless because of lack of love, emotional
security, stable and close relationships, fixed points and
roots.

'(I'm not homeless) from the point of view I haven't
got a bed - I can stay at the reception centres for
weeks.   It's I don't know many people.   I find London
a lonely place.' (WERC male)

'I don't have a home.   Even a flat isn't a home.   A
home is where you have a family.   Technically I've
been homeless for years.' (WERC male)

For the majority, the major factor in deciding whether
or not they were homeless tended to be accommodation, although homelessness was often seen as a composite state
involving such factors as having no employment or money
and implying inadequacy, shame and loneliness or sometimes
a way of life, state of mind, an 'experience':

'I've got to see myself as homeless; no job; no
money; it's like begging, staying at a place like
that.' (WERC male)

Another male, talking about having no job:

'It hurts my pride as a man.'

One male said he was homeless but added:

> 'I am my home, it doesn't worry me, it's an experi-
> ence.'

Another male:

> 'I like to keep moving.   It's good to see how the
> other half live.'

Two subjects no longer saw themselves as homeless, having
secured jobs.

Four females linked homelessness to being unable/un-
willing to return to parents: three claimed they would
not be accepted at home and the other refused to return
because of conflicts.   One male could not return home
because he was a fugitive from sectarian violence in Northern Ireland and another because he had absconded from
psychiatric hospital.

Ten males and three females felt they were not homeless
because if they failed to find accommodation in London
they had a place elsewhere.   In the case of ten (eight
males and two females) this fall-back accommodation was a
parental home:

> 'I can go back home.   I've no need to be homeless.'
> (male)

> 'I've got a home to go back to.' (male)

> 'Down and out but not homeless - I can always go back
> to my parents' home.' (male)

Of the remaining three, one male regarded his friends'
house as his 'home'.   The other male replied:

> 'When you've got friends you're not homeless - my
> friends would always put me up and buy me a drink.'

The female who was fifteen and had run away from home said
she was not homeless:

> 'I can go and live with my mum - not my real mum, my
> friend's mum.'

As it turned out, she would not have been accepted by her
friend's mum and felt rather relieved a week later to be
picked up by the police and returned to her 'real mum'.

Two males were ambivalent about the term homeless,
making geographical distinctions:

'I'm homeless down here - but I've got a home up North
with my wife.'

'I'm not very homeless now.   I could always go home
(parents) or to relatives.   I'm homeless because I
want to be.'

Whether the rest of the sample (fifty-four of the
yeses, ten of the noes) saw themselves as homeless or not
depended on views of their accommodation situation in
London.   Most regarding themselves as homeless linked it
with staying in emergency accommodation and wanting to
graduate to a flat, squat, or living-in job.
   Of the ten noes, four males and three females did not
regard themselves as homeless because they were staying in
the selected projects:

'I can't be homeless if I've got somewhere to go.'
(North male)

'North is my home.' (North male)

One female said that their (her husband and herself)
home was a tent.   They were about to commence a world
tour and were staying in London to collect the necessary
visas.   One male and female felt confident of getting a
place to stay and so were not homeless.   The male felt
certain of getting a living-in job the next day.   The
female asserted:

'If you really want to get a place you will.'

THE EXPERIENCE OF 'HOMELESSNESS'

Being homeless sometimes meant shame and inadequacy:

'I'm annoyed to have to come to a place like this ...
it feels like sinking right down.   I feel inadequate
because I can't take care of myself.' (Centrepoint
male)

'I don't think there's any further down I can get.   I
feel down emotionally and socially.   When you walk
into a cafe they look at you as if you're going to
pinch something.   At the SS [social security] place
they treat you with no feeling whatsoever.' (male)

Some subjects saw a positive status to being homeless.

A few regarded themselves as 'travellers' or 'wanderers'.
For them it represented a state of freedom, a chance to
gain unusual experience:

'I've slept in Regent's Park for six weeks - it didn't
bother me.'

'I'm doing what I want to do.   Meeting unconventional
people and enjoying myself.'

'I'm having a good time and enjoying the adventure.'

Home did not always have a positive connotation.   One
motivation in many was to get away:

'I'm not homesick.   I'd rather be away from home than
stick at home.'

Some females presented themselves and their experience
in a variety of different guises.   They seemed to enjoy
flouting convention and the shock they might cause in
others:

'I'm enjoying being wicked.'

'I'm getting new experiences especially in sex.'

This minority seeing homelessness in a positive light
contrasted starkly with the fire and brimstone views of
the projects.   However, where subjects were content, it
seemed that they were cushioned by recent arrival and the
capacity to suspend anxiety about what might happen
tomorrow:

'That worries me being without a home.   It's not a
nice feeling knowing you might be walking the streets.
But I haven't felt that yet because I've had somewhere
to go.   It may be different tomorrow.'

Being homeless meant 'no security' to one sixteen-year-old
girl, but:

'I don't mind that: I'm quite happy in my present
state ... I came for the experience and I've had a lot
of that.   When I go home I'll freak out at my friends
with clothes from Biba's and tales of what I've done.'

London provided compensations other than Biba's:

'enjoying the bright lights'

'nice to be in the centre of it all'

'I'll never be short of fellas here.'

Whilst others were more critical:

'expensive and hostile place'

'London is full of hustlers.'

'Everyone is out for themselves here.'

Other subjects described the complexity of shifting colours and feelings about their situation, varying almost minute by minute and fitting into none of the homeless models:

'One minute I'm happy, the next I feel shall I go home?   I'm happy when I'm on the brink of getting a job, when I've got food inside me, when I'm meeting new people and as long as I've got a roof over my head.' (Centrepoint male)

Compared with the voluntary societies' and statutory bodies' conception of homelessness as mostly negative, our subjects had more complex views.   We classified them according to whether their total experience in London (up to the initial interview) was mainly positive or negative.

TABLE 4.3 Feelings about the total experience in London whilst homeless

	Males	Females
Largely positive	7	6
More positive than negative	15	14
Mostly negative with some positive	23	9
Almost entirely negative	27	6
Total	72	35

Largely positive: (Centrepoint male) 'What more perfect freedom than walking down the road without a care in the world except worrying where your next meal comes from ... I can smoke and swear when I like ... I'm seeing how the other half live ... seeking new faces, meeting new people....   It's a good experience, you make friends.'

More positive than negative: (gay male) 'I feel a little
disheartened today because I had to walk everywhere, but
otherwise I'm happy.   It takes a lot to make me depressed
and I don't give in easy ... I like the pace of London,
the night life ... gay people here are friendly ... other
Londoners are not friendly and open.'
Mostly negative but with some positive: (male) 'Time
drags, there's not much to do ... people look at you as if
you're a hustler, thief or addict [he was all three] ...
[but] I enjoy walking around seeing the sights.'
Almost entirely negative: (female) 'A frightful experience ... to think that when it's drawing dark you've nowhere to go.   You see hundreds of people and you think -
they've got somewhere, they're OK, look at me, I've got
nowhere ... I am very depressed, sometimes I just sit and
cry.   I can't help it.   I had nothing to eat for three
days.'
(Male) 'I hope I'm going to wake up soon, and this will be
a bad dream.'
   This classification is very arbitrary.   Their focus
was not necessarily on the homeless experience.   If they
had recently experienced sleeping rough in London (twenty-
eight out of seventy-two males, fifteen out of thirty-five
females) this often heavily coloured their over-all view.
Except for a small minority who were accustomed to it,
subjects usually found it a harsh and sometimes shattering
experience, especially in winter:

   'When I was sleeping rough I really felt bad, like
   going home ... but now I have a job, I feel OK.' (male)

   'But when you're hungry you feel like screwing something ... to get caught and put inside - you're all
   right inside ... I couldn't sleep out again.   If I
   thought I had to I'd do something and get put away.
   I'm on the verge of doing something in this place
   (WERC).' (male)

The latter stole a watch in Dover a few days later and
gave himself up to the police.
   Our subjects were usually relatively new to the experience of being homeless in London.   Thirty-nine per cent
of males and 52 per cent of females had been in London for
two nights or less when interviewed and 57 per cent of
males and 63 per cent of females had been there less than
a week.   First impressions were often misleading.   One
girl interviewed on her first night had found both London
and Centrepoint 'great'.   Her reaction was more mixed two
weeks later after dossing about and sitting in all-night
cafés and sleazy clubs.

Our follow-up interviews showed that when the novelty
wore off, subjects viewed the experience less positively.
One girl enjoyed her first homeless experience in London,
but on returning after two weeks at home, she felt 'des-
perately lonely' on being refused admission to Centrepoint
and took a drug overdose in her hostel room.

The main experiences rated as positive by subjects were
the excitement of meeting new people; unconventionality
like meeting dossers; the challenge of surviving and
learning new social skills like begging; the freedom of
being away from the parental home; the 'lights' and
'sights' of London; the bigness of London and 'being at
the centre of things'; benefits of homeless accommodation
particularly Centrepoint and North were often highly
rated.

The main negative experiences were loneliness and
deprivation of sleeping rough and walking the streets
(cold, hungry and 'feeling down and out'); the shame of
feeling inadequate and having to ask for help; the pace,
confusion and hostility of a large city; the cost of food
and accommodation; other homeless people who were 'ex-
cons', 'bums', 'derelict people' ('I've met no one I can
trust'); and the unsatisfactory nature of some residential provision.

MODELS OF HOMELESS YOUNG PEOPLE

The various images held by workers in the homeless field
are important parts of the setting of our research.   They
shape the way the 'problem' is defined and responded to
both in everyday interactions and formal policy.   These
images or models also influenced the questions we asked
about the phenomenon.   As Peter Archard noted: 'All too
frequently, sociologists undertaking studies of deviant
behaviour lay emphasis on the world of the deviant but
fail to incorporate official definitions of the phenomena
they are describing and explaining.' (1)

From analysis of the literature and in talking to
workers in many agencies we identified five models of
homelessness:
1   Individual culpability
2   Political
3   Spiritual/religious
4   Pathological
5   Child
We describe these in detail and compare them with the
views of the subjects.

Individual culpability

This image sees homeless young people as individually
culpable for their condition and behaviour.   The homeless
person has chosen to be destitute and deviant.   He is
perverse or selfish rather than pathological or a victim
of circumstances.   He seeks to evade the rules and obli-
gations of a responsible member of society and corrupts
others either by design or example.   He is classed as a
malingerer, wastrel or criminal, as work-shy, improvident,
contaminated, decadent or malevolent.   Homelessness results from his weakness of character and lack of moral
fibre.

William Rees-Davies, MP, described the Housing (Homeless Persons) Bill as 'a charter for the rent dodger, for
the scrounger, and for the encouragement of the home-
leaver'.   He went on to express concern about new arrivals who 'come off the beach' and 'make themselves homeless' in his seaside constituency of Thanet ('Hansard',
18 February 1977).

In official policy-making, this model, long influential, has been squeezed out.   The punitive ethos of the
casual ward has been replaced by the 'resettlement' philosophy of the reception centre, although some social
security counter clerks, reception centre staff and
policemen still seem to use this model.

This model does accord to young people the status of
self-determination.   However, it lacks compassion,
empathy and any appreciation of the roles of economic and
social inequalities.   It is tied to narrow, conformist
and moralistic notions of how individuals ought to be.
As the Director of CHAR eloquently put it:

> Concentration on single people without homes as
> deviants ... obscures the lack of fundamental rights
> which seriously affects the homeless poor.   (Nick
> Beacock, 'New Horizon Annual Report', 1974)

The individual culpability model not only provides a
framework for blaming, punishing and controlling deviant
individuals, but also a formula for attempts to change
them.   Individuals are cajoled, bullied or enticed into
'decent' citizenship.   For example, one social security
clerk told us that homeless youngsters were deliberately
sent to Salvation Army hostels as a 'short, sharp shock'
(to deter further destitution).   Since individuals are
viewed as lacking 'willpower' and 'self-discipline', the
imposition of external discipline is justified.

Individual culpability was the only model relating to

any sizeable proportion of our subjects' declared experience.   The themes of assuming responsibility and justifi-
cation seemed important.

Sixteen males (22 per cent) and three females (9 per
cent) felt ashamed of being homeless or destitute and at
the implied inadequacy, dependency or degeneracy.   Among
these the general feeling was that they had been 'stupid'
or 'silly' in coming to London either unprepared or with
unrealistically high expectations:

'I normally change my clothes once every other day -
you can't do that here.   I feel terrible.   I felt
embarrassed when I went to Centrepoint - really silly.
The girls [volunteers] ask you questions.   I felt a
fool sitting there - no money ... nothing.' (male)

'I feel silly.   I'm ashamed of begging from these
places (agencies).' (male)

'You can tell I don't belong here, can't you? ... I
hate having to ponce off people.' (female)

Others felt the need to justify being destitute.   They
seemed to want to present themselves as respectable and
self-sufficient, and to defend themselves against charges
of improvidence.   Tales of stolen or lost money shortly
after arrival or en route reflected this concern.   Seven
subjects made such claims.   At least some were probably
fabricated.   Another extenuation took the form of
declaring an intent to seek work and be self-reliant:

'I'm not a layabout.   I'm not going to live off the
state.' (male)

'Everyone has to come down once in their life but I
reckon I've got what it takes to get out of it.   I'm
prepared to work; to do anything.' (male)

Others justified homelessness as a social exploration;
'gaining experience':

'I'm happy to have had the experience.   I've learned
what other people are like ... [and] I've learned about
myself and drugs.' (male aged fifteen)

'I enjoy begging - seeing how much I get.' (female)

Seven females and one male inverted the individual culpability model by seeing naughtiness as positive.   They

flouted conventions and got some satisfaction in shocking
social workers and other parental figures.   Their sense
of devilry came both from being homeless and in three
cases from deviant acts like taking drugs and petty
thieving.   Four of these females derived a similar excitement from running away from home and feeling that the
police were seeking them.

> 'I just do it [housebreaking and petty crime] for the
> hell of it; because I feel like it; maybe it's the
> challenge, I don't know.   It's mostly for kicks, I
> suppose.' (eighteen-year-old girl who talked of being a
> 'non-conformist')

> 'It's all right sleeping rough once you get used to it.
> I talk to the dossers, they tell me all kinds of
> things ... they like you to listen to them and they
> tell you where to go.   It's good being here - I meet
> lots of boys.   I've been terrible really.   At home,
> my mother kept me in at night.' (fifteen-year-old girl)

All of these acknowledged responsibility for their
deviant acts or intentions.   A sixteen-year-old girl complained that teachers never credited her with responsibility:

> 'We [including a friend whom she had run away with]
> were the naughtiest girls in the school. I had the cane
> more than anyone else; I never had me a good report.
> It makes me really fed up they don't do nothing.   They
> feel sorry for me.   They tell me I'm easily led.   I
> do my nut over it.   I'm not.   It's up to me what I
> do.   I've got a mind of my own.   I get in as much
> trouble as I can.'

Another girl, aged fifteen, said she found the discipline at school frustratingly insufficient:

> 'I used to muck about a lot ... the teachers were too
> soft ... they should bring back the cane.'

She enjoyed the romance and drama of running away from
home and 'mixing with dossers', 'sleeping rough', 'smoking
dope' and 'picking up boys'.

> 'I think everyone has to run away from home; it
> teaches you things.   I'm glad I had the guts.   Some
> girls are really sheltered, never do anything.   I'd
> hate to be like that.'

However, for a large proportion, taking or denying
responsibility for destitution or homelessness did not
appear relevant.   It either had to be suffered or even,
in a few cases, enjoyed.   They adopted a fatalistic here-
and-now stance as opposed to the there-and-then stance of
justifying their situation by reference to past events or
future intent to reform:

'I just take things as they come.' (male)

'It's just like everything else.   If you worry about
it, it gets on top of you.' (male)

'It's just like fate controlling me.   You have to take
the rough with the smooth.   I have learned my lesson
and I've enjoyed myself.   I think it was fate I didn't
find a job.' (female)

'You've got to take the good with the bad.' (male)

'It's impossible to look to the future.   Something can
happen to change it all.' (male)

Political

Here the important factors are political, social and economic rather than personal.   The emphasis is on the
social context of actions rather than on the actor.
Factors involved include an acute shortage of suitably
priced accommodation;   unemployment and job scarcity and
the impoverished nature of the environments where young
people live.   Youngsters leave their home towns to gain
independence from their parents, to seek reasonable accommodation and employment and a more stimulating environment, but lack information, contacts and savings, marketable skills or educational qualifications and consequently
a proportion find themselves destitute.

Housing problems are a striking example of a source of
stress to the individual which springs from the inadequacies of the system rather than from his own pathology (Tower Hamlets Case Con., 'The Great East End Housing Disaster', 1973).

Attempts to construct typologies about the nature of
homeless people are a way of evading administrative and
political responsibility for changing the housing situation.   If people are damaged that must not deny their

essential right to accommodation, and damage may be largely a consequence of economic deprivation and criminal and
psychiatric processing. The emphasis is on the rights of
the individual rather than on his responsibilities:

> CHAR sees homelessness as being fundamentally a mani-
> festation of housing failure. Obviously many people,
> both housed and homeless, have social service and medi-
> cal needs, but homeless people with those needs require
> first and foremost, accommodation. It is CHAR's job
> ... to remove the labels which have supplied successive
> governments and local authorities with excuses for
> their failure to respond to the plight of the homeless.
> 'Deviant', 'abnormal', 'psychopathic', 'misfit' - des-
> criptive language which now seems to be a kind of ploy,
> a means of explaining away the total failure of our
> society to house people in decent homes. (Anne Davies,
> Asst Director of CHAR, 'New Horizon Annual Report',
> 1974-5)

These labels are also seen as self-fulfilling:

> 'If young people have no house and job, they are
> labelled as social misfits. They are given a view of
> themselves to which they conform merely because little
> else is expected of them'. (June Lightfoot, CHAR, 1976)

The fundamental problem lies in providing accommodation
primarily in urban centres. Personalities, attitudes,
social relationships and histories of homeless young
people are seen as similar to those of people with homes
or the differences as not being of primary importance.
The young homeless are trapped in a vicious circle.
Their lack of a settled address provides a barrier to
employment or social security; their lack of privacy
lowers immunity to arrest.
   Their life-style is inherently stressful. Social and
economic factors make it more likely that individuals will
feel or appear disturbed and that various needs will force
contact with stigmatising processes like the social services or the police. Many non-homeless people have personal problems but are less socially visible than those in
non-conventional accommodation.
   Only three subjects had an explicitly formulated political perspective on their situation - all males:

> 'I want the whole system to collapse. I don't need to
> work. I hope the country will come to a standstill.
> I can't understand capitalism.'

One male at his re-interview gave us a short paper attack-
ing psychiatric hospitals, written from his own experience
as a patient:

> People come and go from psychiatric hospitals these
> days ... this I suppose is a triggered, delayed reac-
> tion to opposing society's stresses and strains....
> It is a great pity that these people though their
> phobias may be slight or their paranoias illusive are
> treated like cattle. Basically the rat race is still
> on and inside these scantily fabricated buildings the
> air of apathy seethes around the chromium utensils with
> disconsolate concern....
> I can certainly tell you what a nervous disposition
> looks like, but no-one can point an insane person out
> ... I believe these so-called psychiatric patients are
> the only ones who are genuinely searching for a better
> world to live in. They can see who and what THEY are
> very clearly and I'm sure you won't be surprised THEY
> can see who and what their nurses are also. The nurse
> and the staff exploit the patients with a smile.

One man was a political activist in the troubles in Northern Ireland. He understood homelessness to be a function of private property owning:

> 'Everyone has a right to be housed. You won't get it
> by waiting around for it ... they don't tell you your
> rights ... you have to fight for it ... it is a work-
> ing-class struggle.'

A large minority of subjects raised specific issues
concerning their London experiences which had some political relevance. 'Not enough is done to help homeless
people.' 'They [WERC staff] treat you like a number.'
'They [WERC] treat you like hares on a greyhound track,
going round and round.'
These specific complaints were usually slotted into a
more general concern about the way people were treated by
officials. A few were political in a sense of active
protest. Three males were ejected from WERC for refusal
to do the chores and that action could be seen as having
political connotations. Another WERC user on being refused admission was recorded as saying:

> 'Mr X wishes his regards and best wishes to the Hitler
> who refused him entry tonight.'

Another girl described her confrontation with social

security officials.   They had refused her and her boyfriend payment and threatened to call the police.   Her
account went:

> 'Get them [the police].   I'm not walking around like
> this.   How would you feel if you were pregnant.   It's
> all right for you, you've got a roof over your head.
> Then the clerk said, "I work for it."   We'd work for
> it if you'd give us the money and give us a chance to
> get a job.'

In most cases subjects did stress structural factors,
referring for example to the lack of jobs and accommodation in their home towns or in London.   However these
were usually seen as requiring individual responses rather
than political solutions.   They were facts of life.

Spiritual/religious

Homelessness is seen as a fall from grace which the
deviant shares, to a greater or lesser extent, with all
human beings.   He is a sinner to be saved through the
love of the Lord Jesus Christ.   For some organisations,
like the Simon Community, he also lives in a sick, uncaring and spiritually bankrupt society which itself does not
heed Christian values and directions.   Homelessness is a
symptom and index of the spiritual impoverishment of our
society.   Spitalfields Crypt project for homeless alcoholics put this model at its most uncompromising:

> The Crypt view is based on the sufficiency of Christ's
> redemption for ... all men, however damaged by sin,
> suffering and contemporary social evils. (Spitalfields
> Crypt, 'Newsletter', Spring 1967)

> Underlying all Salvation Army endeavours is its domi-
> nant interest in the spiritual welfare of people.
> Salvationists believe that regeneration is more impor-
> tant than rehabilitation. ('Salvation Army Annual
> Report', 1976)

This model was a dominant force in the development of
missionary work to the destitute in the nineteenth century.   Originally the Salvation Army took a dogmatically
religious stance which has now been partly concealed by
social work and psychiatric ideologies.   Peter Archard
writes:

Increasingly, missions and Christian charities combine
their missionary work with definitions of habitual
drunkenness that seek answers in professional social
work and psychiatry. The human 'sciences' are invoked
to fortify their moral standpoint and Christian-based
skid row projects employ social workers, doctors, and
psychiatrists. ('The Bottle Won't Leave You', Alcoholics
Recovery Project, 1975)

In this model, help is a form of charity to which the
subject has no special right.   Economic and social
forces, as in the first model, play little part.   Although the subject is destitute and homeless, the primary
concern is with his spiritual development.   Soup, bread
and shelter is a way of bringing him to the Lord.   Some
projects hold regular services and Bible readings for
residents; some have chapels attached to the hostel or
community.   Emphasis is placed on salvation and redemp-
tion; some projects have a 'prodigal son' philosophy.
We met one young man who had been 'converted' twenty-seven
times: a lot of fatted calves!
There were five males with a religious perspective on
their experiences.   One said he had come to London to
'witness for the Lord....   Yes (I'm homeless) down here
but not destitute because I've got the Lord.   In earthly
matters I am - I've got no money or job.'   At his re-
interview we found that this perspective had evaporated.
His main reason for coming to London had been re-formula-
ted as 'to escape myself and my responsibilities' (his
wife and children).
One male in the Divine Light movement saw his homelessness as part of his search to find himself:

'It's your own decision to be on the road, you know it
will be difficult.   Pleasure is transitory.   One
shouldn't indulge one's senses, it hinders your experiences.   This is NIRVANA, everything is here, inside is
where it is.   I am my home, it's a test I must go
through before I get where I'm heading for.   I'm heading for completeness, perfection.   I'm not the doer,
the force takes me.   It's a game that GOD has set out
for you.'

Two of the others related their experience to God.
One had wanted to be a priest until told that he was ban-
ished from the Church after assaulting a priest by 'pull-
ing his buttons off'.   The other claimed to be a 'black
magician' and avoided any hostels with a Christian bias
such as Centrepoint and the Salvation Army, seeing them as
'dangerous and corrupt'.

Pathological

In this perspective homeless people are seen as socially
inadequate, maladjusted and psychologically disturbed.
The problems are much broader and less tangible than lack
of accommodation and there is a need for counselling, befriending and even psychiatric treatment.   They are unem-
ployable rather than unemployed;   unhousable rather than
unhoused;   unable to form relationships rather than simply
alone.   As in the spiritual model, the environment may be
seen as an essentially destructive place affording little
possibility for gaining health.

> Many young people who come to London have already to
> some degree suffered damage - emotional deprivation,
> split families or stressful situations.... In the
> majority of cases they are perilously ill-equipped to
> deal with the pressures that they will find in the par-
> ticular culture of the West End of London. ('Centrepoint
> Annual Report', April 1971)

> The inability to express love seems to be the greatest
> single feature of the young drifter.(Gordon Batten,
> 'Rink Club Social Survey', 1968)

This particular model has dominated research in the
field since the 1930s. (2)   As in the individual culpability model, the values of conformity, routine, self-
control and stability are stressed and equated with adequacy and wholeness.   Deviations are seen as symptoms of
maladjustment, disturbance and mental instability.   Homeless young people have casual, superficial and manipula-
tive social relations and their backgrounds reflect a high
instance of deviant behaviour including criminality, drug
and alcohol abuse and sexual promiscuity.

> Homelessness and destitution certainly head our list of
> presenting problems but in almost all cases analysis
> has revealed many other contributing factors.   We are,
> for example, particularly concerned by the development
> of illegal squatting amongst young people and the
> numerous problems generated as a result of that way of
> life ('GALS Annual Report', 1976).

It provides a stark contrast with the political model.
The individual is not held centrally responsible for his
behaviour but is seen as acting out pathological propensi-
ties.   The cause is located in his background or genetic
make-up;   such factors as disruption or emotional depriva-

tion in childhood are viewed as particularly pathogenic.
This model dismisses the individual's behaviour as irra-
tional, disturbed and purposeless in contrast to the behaviour of the helper.
   When this model is translated into the helping process
there seem to be two major dangers. The helper is licen-
sed to over-rule the client's assessment of himself and
also to impose certain values rather than simply give him
space to be and to learn. Second, the client may inter-
nalise a fundamentally pessimistic and deterministic view
of himself which can undermine his own capacity for self-
help and self-direction.
   We had postulated that many subjects would disclaim
responsibility for their behaviour or present situation by
using a pathological framework. Few did.
   Only six subjects, all males, explicitly and extensively disclaimed responsibility within a pathological framework. One, aged eighteen, saw himself as subject to un-
controllable urges to assault people and to steal:

   'When I get the drink in me ... my hands just shivers,
   I have to grab on to something ... I just feel like
   choking something, squeezing until I feel back to
   normal and I can walk off happy again....   That's why
   I never get drunk because I'm afraid that if I take
   over two pints and have an argument with someone I
   might be the cause of their death....   The hands do
   go, the whole lot goes ... you just have to do it.'

   'I don't want to do it (burglary), I have to do it.
   I need help, I need help bad.   I need something done
   to my brain.'

He described himself as the 'black sheep of the family'
and an 'incorrigible rogue' but was one of our wittiest
subjects.   He had spent most of his life since eight in
institutions.
   Another male blamed drink, fate and his childhood and
'something wrong with his brain' for crimes of sexual
assault.

   'It's a deep psychological something.   I can track it
   back to when I was thirteen years old.'

In the follow-up interview, in jail for rape, he described
himself as a 'psychopath'.
   A twenty-three-year-old blamed his unstable, unloving
background and his colour (half-caste) for his developing
homosexual tendencies, inability to cope with life, and

feeling unable to go on.   Suicide seemed the only way out
as people, mostly psychiatrists, police and friends, were
always 'getting at him':

> 'They've picked on me since I was twelve.   They've put
> me in a set environment and they're watching me.   They
> want to make me cry again ... I don't want to take it
> any more going on for years.   I can't stand it any
> more.'

This young man was illegitimate and had been rejected by
his mother and brought up by an aunt.   He had been in and
out of psychiatric in-patient care since he was twelve and
in prisons since hw was eighteen.
    Another male saw himself as liable to erupt violently
under the influence of drink - 'to lose my head'.   He
claimed no control over this.   At the time of the interview, he was on the run from psychiatric care.
    A further nine males and nine females claimed that
their background or some inherent factor had adversely
affected their personality.   They were prepared to accept
a large measure of responsibility for actions but saw some
factor as being influential in their present situation:

> 'I know it's partly my fault, but foster parents had
> ruined me.   It's fifty-fifty really.' (girl explaining
> why she was a dosser)

One fifteen-year-old girl talked of her 'funny bits':

> 'If someone bugs me, I really go at them.   It's like a
> temper, it takes a lot to get going, but once it's
> going it really goes.'

This was largely sparked off by her father who didn't like
her and favoured her sister.   She didn't take to him because 'I'm not sure he's really my Dad.'   It was a question of leaving home or 'going mad.   I'm nearly mad now.'
    One sixteen-year-old female discussed her 'psychologi-
cal problems' at length.   'I've got a split personality.'
She was 'extroverted and popular' at school but 'took it
out on the family at home'.   She wanted to get her O
levels, but was 'addicted to skiving'.   She had a 'mas-
sive inferiority complex' and described the psychiatrists
at the Young People's Unit from which she had just absconded as 'egocentric pigs'.   They 'analysed everything you
said' and 'it's a load of crap'.   She was very self-ana-
lytical and one moment accepted the psychiatric assessment
which in the next was 'crap'.   The Unit told her she was

'out of control', 'resented authority', 'lived up in a
cloud', and 'let her mother walk all over her'.

Several others mentioned having 'psychological problems', 'depression' or 'nerves' but did not use this to
disclaim responsibility. A few others mentioned as
reasons for leaving home, conflicts with parents but did
not seem to view these as affecting their personality.

Most of these explicitly accepting or ambivalent about
the pathological model had had contact with psychiatric
services.   This was also true of those rejecting it.
Two males and two females rejected the model after being
in mental hospital:

> 'I don't think I know what they (psychiatrists) are
> talking about.   I'm not mad.   I get a bit mad some-
> times and go a bit queer, but then everybody does,
> don't they?' (female)

One male aged twenty-four still resented his mother for
authorising electric shock treatment at the age of sixteen:

> 'That can really bugger you up, it can damage your
> brain - it made me worse and worse.'

He maintained that there was nothing wrong with him.   He
spent periods in psychiatric hospitals simply pretending
to take the pills.   He did not feel his mother had
damaged him.   She had been and was simply making life
more painful and difficult.

One male aged twenty-one who had had extensive contact
with the social services said his childhood had been 'a
turmoil'.   His father died when he was four and he was
'in and out of children's homes'; his mother was always
doing 'moonlight flits'.   He said that the courts and
probation officers 'all believe my background affected me'
but 'I don't believe that rubbish - you're either a thief
or not.'   However he 'plays along with them' to get reduced sentences when up for trial.   He placed a very different interpretation on his background: 'My childhood
wasn't happy but it was not disturbed either.   It taught
me to stand on my own two feet.'

One female said her social worker was 'always saying
how depressed I am.   I don't think I'm half as depressed
as what she says I am.'   Another female said of social
workers:

> 'They're always asking you a load of stupid questions.
> I don't understand half the words they're saying.'

One index of how closely our subjects were aligned to
the pathological model lay in their response to the word
'problem'.

TABLE 4.4   Subjects' response to 'Have you any problems?'

	Males	Females
Yes	44	17
No	18	8
Ambivalent	4	4
Question not asked	6	6
Total	72	35

Of the males asked the question, 67 per cent replied
'yes', 27 per cent answered 'no'.   Of the females, 59 per
cent replied 'yes' and 28 per cent 'no'.   Of the male
'yeses', nineteen gave the lack of or need to find accommodation, job and/or money as their only 'problem'.   The
remainder usually referred to these factors.   However,
only eight gave as a 'problem' a general psychological
state.   For instance:

'My nerves, that's all.'

'It's my fits.'

A further male replied that he was 'financially embarrassed' adding 'I may have problems mentally, but that's to
be decided' and referred to a tendency to 'depression and
nerves occasionally'.

For the other males, 'problems' concerned specific
others or their social situation in London – missing their
friends at home, the problem of getting a girlfriend, etc.
One male had a 'family problem – not getting on with my
parents' as well as 'the problem of my clothes – if I go
for a job I want to look decent'.   Another said about his
problems: 'keeping good care of my wife – she's decent
and respectable'.   Another male had a problem 'with my
girlfriend'.

On the whole, females stressed economic problems less
than males.   Of female affirmatives, five gave accommodation, jobs and/or money as their only 'problems'.   Only
four females gave psychological or emotional states as a
problem.

'I've got psychological problems.   I don't think I
could keep a steady job.   I'm scared of getting a
job.'

'Only overcoming my history.   I've got to become a
bigger person.'

Two females said they had problems but didn't know what
they were.   One other female implicitly replied 'yes':

'I don't want to be rude but I can sort out my own
problems, thank you.   I don't want sympathy.   I hate
sympathy.'

For the other five females their problems were either
focused on specific others ('a husband problem' or concern
'about mother's health') or on practical questions.   Two
of them included lack of accommodation:

'Only that I'm pregnant - I don't know where I am going
to be when I have the baby.'

'A reading problem - it makes it difficult to find a
hostel place.'

The 'noes' sometimes responded facetiously or were em-
phatic in their denials:

'I don't see being homeless as a problem.' (male)

'Not that I know of [laugh].' (male)

'Not really - the worst problem I've got at the moment
is to find a light for my cigarette.' (male)

The question seemed to discourage further communication - as if they were responding by refusing to cate-
gorise heartfelt difficulties into the 'problem' category.
'Problem' seemed to imply something 'mental' or permanent
or insurmountable unless it was connected with money or
finding employment.   There was a strong tendency to
assure us that any 'problems' were minor, temporary, ex-
trinsic and under control:

'Just no money and nowhere to stay - when I get some
money, I'll be all right.' (male)

'Only my kid being in hospital - worrying about him is
the only problem I've got.' (male)

Child

This model plays on the notion of youth as being one
remove from childhood.   Terms like 'naive', 'impulsive',
'adrift', 'at risk' and 'vulnerable' are used to convey
childlike qualities.   These young people leave home im-
pulsively, lured by a romantic and unrealistic picture of
London or driven by a desperate need to escape from home.

> They are most vulnerable to all the evil forces that
> unfortunately exist in our great capital city. (Sir
> Maurice Laing, Introduction to 'Centrepoint Annual
> Report', 1975)

They are straws in the wind, easily blown about by sini-
ster and destructive forces which will manipulate their
half-formed minds and young bodies.   They are taken over
by powerful forces: 'Come here and let me see your pretty
beads dear'.
    As in the pathology model, impotence, dependence and
diminished responsibility are implied in contrast to the
mature objectivity of the observer.   However, it does
this by reference to immaturity rather than pathology and
avoids the stigmatic process attached to deviancy labels.
The individual is viewed as normal for his age or, at
worst, developmentally retarded.   This retardation is
phasal or surmountable given support, guidance and a fav-
ourable environment.

> On leaving home a young person is likely to be in a
> state of great emotion and excitement.   Realisation of
> some of the difficulties and loneliness of life in
> London and other large cities may take some weeks and
> it is during this period that he or she is most vulner-
> able to exploitation.   Quite a number want to return
> home after two or three weeks, having made their ges-
> ture of independence. (DHSS, 'Working Group on Homeless
> Young People', July 1976, HMSO)

These young people have to be rescued from possible exploitation within a destructive environment.   The key
words are vulnerable, exploitation and gesture.   They
persist in seeking illusions rather than solid reality.

> The number of wicked step-parents or Victorian-type
> fathers who can not get on with their daughters (never
> the other way round) and turn them out is beyond belief
> but, due to their youth and inexperience they cannot
> appreciate that loving concern takes many forms. (Brenda
> Rayson, 'Girls at Risk')

Few subjects expressed views endorsing this model.
Three girls felt vulnerable to sexual assaults. Very few
admitted to feeling at risk although some noted the dangers of the 'big city':   'full of hustlers' and 'it's
like a web if you're not careful'. Most felt they were
careful and strong enough to avoid these dangers. But
one male decided to return home immediately after seeing
'a guy on drugs who looked like he was dying. That could
happen to me.'
Leaving home for London was often seen as a reaction
against parental authority. They mentioned their desire
for 'freedom' and 'independence'. One girl, aged sixteen, said she left home because 'I wasn't allowed to
drink, smoke or swear.' She liked being in London because 'you can do what you want to'.
One male and four females explicitly aligned themselves
with the child model at some point or another. A girl
of fifteen asked if she had any problems:

'I'm slattered in them. What shall I do next...?
I'm really scared, I mean I'm out in the big world,
fifteen and on my own ... I want to go home but I don't
want to go home. I don't want to go because I know
what it's like at home but I don't want my mum to
worry. I'm going to start crying in a moment ... I
need someone a lot older and wiser than me to sort them
out.'

A male, aged seventeen, who left a community home at fifteen said:

'They [child care authorities] don't tell you what to
do, how to look after yourself, they just let you out.'

An eighteen-year-old girl said:

'I'm sure half of me isn't grown up. I'm not as wise
as I should be. All I want to do really is to go
home. I'm a homeless, friendless, fatherless waif ...
I'd like to be a woman, but I'm only a girl. I'd like
to be more shrewd. I trust people too easily.'

DISSONANCE

Comparison of the agencies' models with the views and experiences of our subjects indicates substantial areas of
dissonance. One group of people are using various dimensions to assess another. As Miller and Paul remind us:

When defining the social problems of the lower class,
it is vital to distinguish between what really are
problems in the lower class community and what appear
to be problems because of an implicit comparison with
features of middle-class culture. (3)

Whereas the agencies theorise and perceive homeless
people in there-and-then frameworks, our subjects were
rooted in the present time.   They were thoroughly heter-
ogeneous and defied restriction within the boundaries of
any possible model.

All the agency models seem basically pessimistic about
the homeless and their environment.   The child model sees
them in a bleak and negative way giving little weight to
their experience and capabilities.   The rest, with the
exception of individual culpability, also see them as
helpless and hapless.   In the political model, economic
forces, over which they can have little influence, push
them from dole queue to night shelter.   In the pathology
version, they are up against the massed forces of their
own internal pathology.   This quotation combines both
pessimistic perspectives:

The individuals [homeless young] were seen to divide
into two broad categories.   The first being made up of
young people who had experienced long periods of unemployment and had come to London looking for work and
accommodation.   We found this group very disturbing as
it was the social and economic climate of their own
home areas which caused them to come to London.   The
second group could be defined as those individuals who
left home because of personal problems which could not
be contained within or tolerated by the home community,
e.g. heavy drinking, difficult relationships with other
members of the family. (The Scots Group, 'Young Scots in
London, WECVS, 1976)

The models are badly infected with moral indignation.
Homelessness is obviously a bad process and someone or
some structural defect is to blame.   They or it must be
dealt with.   Both workers and agencies define themselves
out of the entire process into their own internal strategies.   Their task is to pick up the pieces, to cater for
those whom everyone else rejects.   In the political
model, the blame is thrown on to the capitalist society
and the agencies implicitly define themselves outside of
that.   The pathologists see the youngsters as defective
and themselves as properly qualified to diagnose and administer to cases of defective functioning.

The relationship between the helper and those he seeks
to help is usually seen as a polarity, with the latter as
dependent, deprived, disorientated and deficient and the
former as self-sufficient, privileged, perceptive and
wholesome, the selfless dispenser of sympathy and solutions.   One subject satirized this view by observing how
the roles are sometimes reversed:

'You know I feel sorry for social workers sometimes ...
some of them need help more than we do.... You have
to give them a good sob story to keep them happy.'

By effectively defining themselves as outside the perceived phenomena, the projects evade the issue of what is
in it for them.   Herschel Prins identifies groups of
factors motivating the helping of others.   He mentions
creativity, voyeurism and curiosity; the unconscious
needs to punish, to be in control, and adequate in the
face of the inadequacy of others; restitution for early
destruction fantasies and aggressive feelings. (4)
     Those of us involved with the young homeless are bound
up in similar processes.   In the young homeless, we may
find a mirror to our own needs and difficulties; counter-
parts to our own feelings of despondency, vulnerability
and impotence.   In a metaphorical sense, we may feel
'homeless': insecure, forsaken, disconnected.   Our
affinity with the young homeless may be based as much on
the parts of ourselves that we repress as on those we
acknowledge.   Through them we may contact the suppressed
sides of ourselves - for instance, the impulsiveness and
abandon kept in check by responsibility and 'concern';
the insecurity and neediness perhaps underlying the self-
possessed and self-sufficient front of the helper.   In
this way we may attend to and experience - if only vicariously - the needs and tendencies that we repress or in-
hibit.   Our images of the young homeless may provide a
way of indirectly acknowledging these, serving as reposi-
tories or dumping grounds for the hidden sides of ourselves.
     Homelessness attracts the do-gooder, the idealist, the
evangelist, the puritan.   The workers in the voluntary
agencies tend to be 'concerned', earnest, moralistic;
governed by a strong sense of responsibility and self-
sacrifice; and inspired or obsessed by the desire to
help, change, protect or save others.   In the young homeless, they perhaps find their perfect complement.
     All the models wrap the complex and individuated exper-
iences of hundreds of young people around one or two central points.   Complex motivation, often obscure to the

homeless young person gets thrown into explanation boxes marked 'SOCIETY' or 'INDIVIDUAL'.   Agencies and workers take fuzzy snapshots of the problem.   They define clients in the ways that they show themselves to the workers and agencies.   Behaviour in a particular day centre or night shelter is seen as a reliable guide and indicator to what will happen elsewhere.   But the snapshot is a photo of both the agency and the user.   If the homeless young person is frightened it may be that he sees something fearful in the project and the staff.

These snapshots grossly oversimplify the homeless situation.   The political model reduces the motives of new-comers and the quality of their homeless experience to economic factors.   The pathological model views their history in terms of clinical significance with little awareness of the personal resources of the potential client.   The individual culpability model scores moral points and the child model stresses danger and vulnerability.   Young people are variously reduced to a pawn in a giant social chess game, a 'victim', a 'case' or 'problem';   a candidate for political representation, treatment, punishment, parenting or salvation.

> The Scots Group were concerned that the lack of facilities - both accommodation and employment - made it very difficult for them to help many of these young people to establish a way of life that was meaningful to them. Lacking such facilities, these young people were in danger of becoming trapped in the West End scene ('Young Scots in London').

But homelessness is not simply negative;   it has positive possibilities as well.   It can be used as a period of mobility, of changing homes, transition and exploration.   To leave home and survive in London might indicate qualities of self-determination, initiative and resourcefulness at least as substantial as walking the Pennine Way.   Some young homeless get jobs and find conventional accommodation.   Even for those who return home it could still have been a growth experience.

> '[I've learned] to fend for myself - it comes hard after living at home for twenty years ... money doesn't go anywhere.   I used to moan at home.   Why didn't I get this [or that] to eat....   You don't realise.... You've got to work if you're to survive or just end up a drop-out.' (male)

> 'London is not all it's cracked up to be....   I don't take things for granted anymore.' (male)

Homeless newcomers, in the main, do not see themselves
as markedly different from other young people. They do
not see the term 'homeless' as saying something about
their characters or personalities. Where differences are
recognised, apart from those few accepting the pathological model, these are viewed as temporary and practical.
Unlike social service workers, they are not much concerned
with who or what is responsible for the situation. They
do not see it as a 'problem' rooted in their past or as
one requiring a political solution. Subjects rarely disclaimed responsibility by blaming their backgrounds or
society. Where they did blame or protest, it was as individuals complaining about the thoughtless actions of
other individuals (parents, officials etc.) rather than as
a part of a disadvantaged group or class aligned against
various bureaucratic structures and vested interests.
Psychological perspectives were not seen as relevant
except by a small minority, usually those who had been in
psychiatric hospital. 'Problem' did not seem a helpful
word to facilitate communication.

The homeless newcomer defines himself as an individual
and places importance on his own abilities and luck and
fate. Energy and attention is focused largely in the
present moment. Anxiety about tomorrow is suspended
while the more immediate situation is either appreciated
or suffered. Planning, beloved and valued by the agencies, is not perceived as crucial; immediate gratification and spontaneity are emphasised as against deferred
gratification and self-control.

Agencies see this as not taking the situation 'seriously', as not being 'realistic' or 'motivated'. However,
the homeless newcomer may not, and often cannot, see
becoming settled as his main priority. He may be intent
on the hour-to-hour business of surviving and where possible enjoying the experience of a new environment. He
may be trying to postpone going back to an unfavourable
situation or having a holiday. By suspending his anxieties and living in the present, he may sustain his morale
and stay alert. The attitudes, qualities and skills
needed to survive in such an extreme environment may be
very different from those in more conventional settings.
As one male said:

'I've learned to survive when I've got nothing.'

Chapter 5

BACKGROUNDS AND ORIGINS

Although much of this chapter concentrates on deviance,
institutional experience and other possible deviations
from the 'norm', we mean no support to the pathological
model, outlined earlier.   We are simply listing various
notable experiences that subjects had had prior to coming
to London.
    Questions about the causes and long-term significance
of such deviations and what they may indicate about their
characters are largely left open.   What may be more significant than deviant behaviour is the labelling and
other processing that follows it.   Deviance may imply
less about the deviant's character than about his social
position and context and in particular the actions of
those responsible for processing him.

FAMILY LIFE AND 'INSTITUTIONAL CARE'

We postulated that a high proportion of our sample would
come from homes broken by the death or departure of one
or both parents.   Tables below show that 46 per cent of
males and 54 per cent of females come from such homes and
that by far the main cause is parental separation.   We
have not counted as 'broken' those cases where the parents
separate or die after the subject becomes sixteen.

TABLE 5.1 Numbers from broken homes

	Males	Females
Homes broken before subject is sixteen	33	19
Homes not broken	38	15
False/highly unreliable data	1	1
Total	72	35

TABLE 5.2   Nature of 'breach' in home

Homes first broken by	Males	Females
Parental separation	22	13
Parental death	9	5
Abandonment at birth/within first year	2	1
Total	33	19

Very few subjects associated the breaking up of the parental marriage with their present situation.   Among these this girl, aged eighteen, made the most explicit connection:

'It's my step-mother's fault I'm in the situation I am now....   She's really horrible - she's only after his (her father's) money ... I'd be living with my father if it wasn't for her....   Since my mother died I've had no love, none that I can see, feel or touch....   I need someone like my father, someone to love'.

Table 5.3 shows that 32 per cent of males and 28.5 per cent of females have experienced institutional care.   By 'institutional care' we mean living in an establishment that under the Children and Young Persons Act (1969) is or is to be classified as a 'community home'.   Included in this category are establishments that were called children's homes, approved schools, training centres, reception and remand centres and remand homes at the time some older members were resident.

TABLE 5.3   Experience of institutional care

	Male	Female
Experience of institutional care	23	10
None	49	25
Total	72	35

We looked at the overlap between broken homes and institutional care:

TABLE 5.4   Numbers from broken homes and/or experience of institutional care

	Male	Female
Broken homes and institutional care	14	8

	Male	Female
Institutional care only	9	2
Broken home only	19	11
Total (Broken home and/or institutional care)	42	21

We evaluated our subjects' views of their family background and where relevant, institutional care:

TABLE 5.5   Overall evaluation of family life

	Males	Females
Mainly positive	25	9
Mixed feelings (or no strong feelings)	17	8
Mainly negative	28	15
No evaluation/non-committal	2	3
Total	72	35

Mainly positive: 'It was a happy family, no problems ...
I miss my little sister.' (male, aged nineteen)
Mixed feelings: 'I miss my mother a lot ... she cares
about me a lot ... friends are not important as long as
I've got my mother.... [Later in interview] I feel at
home with her for a day or two, then we'd be arguing and
I'd be off again.   I'd think: it's the same as always.'
(female, aged seventeen).
Mainly negative: 'My mother was a compulsive gambler, my
father was an alcoholic - he'd never talk to you except to
give you his backhand ... there were rows every Saturday
night ... we went hungry and went to school in social
security clothes....   It was hell [laughs] - it wasn't
a home life ... I've always been fighting to stay above
because of my parents sinking right down' (male, aged
twenty-two).

TABLE 5.6   Overall evaluation of institutional care

	Males	Females
Mainly positive	6	5
Mixed feelings (or no strong feelings)	7	1
Mainly negative	8	4
No evaluation	2	-
Total	23	10

Reactions to community homes varied from a 'nightmare' to a sense of relief to be away from an unhappy home:

'They (the courts and parents) were writing me off as a delinquent....   It was terrible ... your first feeling is "Why am I here?"   It's like a nightmare - you wake up and you're in a school.' (male, aged twenty-two)

'The best years of my life - you knew you were looked after ... I was a tearaway before ... out of hand ... it settled me down.' (male, aged twenty)

Some had mixed feelings, as with this female, aged seventeen, who actually chose to be 'put away':

'I wanted to get put away in a home, so I got my mother to take me down to the welfare....   It wasn't really better than being at the house, but I'd rather be in the [community] home than in the house with all that drinking and fighting.'

Experiences depended on the particular regime of the institution sent to:

'It [the second home] was different - you weren't hit with a stick ... lots of toys ... I was happy there but not as happy as with my mother' (male, aged twenty).

'It made me so I can't stand any kind of authority ... there were some really tough girls in there - they used to say: if you don't shut up I'll stick a fag end up your nose and things like that' (female, aged eighteen).

'I kept breaking out 'cos I didn't want to be shut up ... I only met robbers there.' (male, aged eighteen)

Some felt it had a positive effect and others a negative one:

'It taught me to live on my own ... I can co-operate more with people than I used to.' (female, aged seventeen)

'I used to be quiet and do anything I was told, but now I'm wild completely. I try to control myself but I can't. I've been locked up and I'm going to get as much freedom as I can ... I don't like to be stuck in one place after being in a home for so many years.' (female, aged seventeen)

One male, aged fifteen, who was absconding from a home
with a therapeutic bias, said, 'I didn't like it ... it's
supposed to be good for you.   I just found it boring.
They had these group meetings ... I found them a waste of
time ... I decided to leave.'

CRIMINAL EXPERIENCE

Table 5.7 shows the extent of 'criminalisation' among our
sample.   We have classified under 'custodial' those who
have served one or more sentences in prison, borstal, detention centres or young offenders' prison;   under
'supervision' those who have been on probation and/or had
a suspended sentence, but have not had a 'custodial' sentence;   and under 'minor' those convicted for an offence
but not given a 'custodial' or 'supervision' sentence.
We do not include in the tables under 'custodial' time
in institutional care as a result of criminal proceedings.

TABLE 5.7   Most serious type of sentence (since sixteen
years old)

Most serious sentence	Males	Females
'Custodial'	23	1
'Supervision'	8	5
'Minor'	15	2
None known	24	24
Not applicable (under 16)	1	3
Refused to give information	1	-
Total	72	35

TABLE 5.8   Most serious type of sentence (since sixteen
years old) by project (males only)

Most serious sentence	Centre-point	WERC	North	All pro-projects
'Custodial'	6	14	3	23
'Supervision'	2	5	1	8
'Minor'	8	6	1	15
None known	11	9	4	24
Not applicable (under 16)	1	-	-	1
Refused information	1	-	-	1
Total	29	34	9	72

Sixty-four per cent of our male sample and 23 per cent of our females had received at least one kind of sentence since the age of sixteen years.   Forty-three per cent of males have received 'custodial' and/or 'supervision' sentences;   32 per cent of the male sample have actually received 'custodial' sentences.   Seventeen per cent of females had been given 'custodial' and/or 'supervision' sentences;   only one (3 per cent) had received a 'custodial' sentence.

Table 5.8 shows that 56 per cent of WERC men have received 'custodial' and/or 'supervision' sentences, compared with only 28 per cent of the Centrepoint men. Centrepoint men tended to be younger than WERC males seven Centrepoint males but none from the reception centre were aged seventeen or under.

We suspect that at least several individuals have understated or concealed their criminal record.   In many cases, we suspected the respondent of hiding something from us;   the difficulty is uncertainty about whether it is a prison stay or a period of unemployment.   One seventeen-year-old male from Centrepoint refused to say whether he had been 'in trouble with the law', but a recent six-month period of his life remained unaccounted for.

For a few subjects at least crime was or had been a career.   Many, however, viewed it either as a phasal development or as a strategy for immediate survival:

'I'm an excellent pickpocket but I wouldn't do it now ... at sixteen you shouldn't be going round battering and mugging and pickpocketing.' (sixteen-year-old female).

'The social wouldn't give me nowt so I went on scrap [stealing lead etc.].' (male, aged seventeen)

Subjects varied from being openly proud of their criminal exploits to being ashamed.

'I'm stupid - easily led.   I'm ashamed of being on probation.' (female)

Several were ambivalent on this score.   One male, for instance, enjoyed relating his criminal adventures but only reluctantly told us he had been in prison because it made him 'look silly'.   Younger subjects in particular might regard crime as romantic and yet still basically 'wrong':

'If we hadn't been starving we wouldn't have done it
[burglary] ... I'm ashamed of what I've done ... I'll
never do it again.... The police say we're worse than
the lads - we do the big places ... I know how to do
it. They [the burglaries] were done professionally
like - no fingerprints [she laughs] - Bonny and Clyde.'
(female, aged seventeen, on bail)

Only a few questioned the basis or workings of the law:

'The law isn't up to my standard. The law over in
Northern Ireland is as bad as a nine bob note.' (male)

'If you can't be a crook, you can't get anywhere. No-
body's honest. Everybody's thieving something - look
at office workers and notepaper.' (male)

The impact of being 'inside' varied. Take two con-
trasting experiences of borstal:

'I hated it. I realised how much I missed my mother
and father, my freedom, what good clothes and food
meant to me ... I buttoned myself down [refused to be
provoked into violence by other inmates] - that's
partly why I hated it so much.'

'It's a doss, too easy, wouldn't learn anybody anything
... time flies ... it quietened me down but it did
nothing for me.... It makes some people worse. What
they don't know when they go in, they do when they come
out ... [after a week] some are already talking about
doing a job when they come out.'

Although several subjects seemed hardened to prison
life, the prospect of going back inside had prompted them
to try to go straight. It was not easy. One male had
partly come to London to avoid the 'bad company' of his
friends. Another said: 'It's better to work (than
steal) - it's doing it though.'
   Quite a few subjects referred to such potentially
mitigating factors as the influence of alcohol, 'bad company' or the need to survive, when explaining their criminal behaviour. However, these were not usually intended
as excuses (although this might partly reflect our accepting and sometimes even fascinated attitude).

'I drink to drown my sorrows, then I go out and do
something [criminal], but I don't get drunk a lot.'
(male, aged twenty).

Few subjects went as far as pleading diminished responsibility.   Three males saw themselves as subject to un-
controllable criminal urges aggravated by drink.   Several
other subjects to lesser degrees accepted or exploited the
notion of diminished responsibility.   For instance:

'I got it lighter [than her friend who got probation]
because I'm in care till eighteen and my children's
home officer was there and he showed them reports.
Some people say that being in a home you should be
better brought up ... but it's worked the opposite with
me ... homes just make you terrible, they make you want
more freedom than you're at.   It's like being locked
up in a prison, you can't have freedom' (seventeen-
year-old female)

'I didn't need to do it [shoplifting in her home town].
I think it was because I was under strain.   If I had
got caught the fact that I was under psychiatric supervision would have got me off.' (female, aged sixteen)

PSYCHIATRIC EXPERIENCE

As the table below shows, 17 per cent of males spent some
time in psychiatric hospital, compared with only 8.6 per
cent of females.   The difference narrows slightly when
including all those receiving psychiatric treatment, including out-patient care, about 19 per cent of the men
compared with 14.2 per cent of women have had such treatment.
   The category 'assessment only' below, includes those
routinely referred for psychiatric assessment while on
remand or in prison.

TABLE 5.9   Psychiatric experience

	Males	Females
In-patient treatment	12	3
Out-patient treatment only	2	2
Assessment only (no treatment)	13	1
None known	45	29
Total	72	35

One project difference may be significant.   Twenty-
four per cent of the WERC men but only 14 per cent of the

Centrepoint men have received psychiatric treatment.
   Those with experience of psychiatric care were usually
critical:

   'They said to me "we're going to send you to a lovely
   place with big games and lovely pictures", and there I
   am all happy about it and all it is is a pack of
   madmen....   They couldn't find nothing wrong with
   me ...' (male, now eighteen, talking of being eight
   and in a child psychiatric unit).

   'They thought I was mad you know ... they asked me to
   sign this thing saying I was leaving [the general hos-
   pital] and I signed away lovely - up in the madhouse I
   went ... I see these fellas running for the door and
   two fellas trying to get out of the window.   I thought
   to myself, I'm bound to take fits if I stay in here.'
   (male)

   'I got fed up.   He [the psychiatrist] asked me nasty
   questions ... the queerest talk ... kept using fancy
   big words ... I didn't know what they were ... I said
   "Yes" that was right, but I hadn't got a clue what they
   were talking about.   I went "Yes, yes, yes," just to
   get it over with.' (male)

OVERLAPS BETWEEN INSTITUTIONAL CARE, CRIMINAL RECORD AND
PSYCHIATRIC TREATMENT

TABLE 5.10   Incidence of criminal and/or psychiatric
processing among subjects experiencing institutional care

	Males	Females
Criminal record only:		
'custodial'	9	1
'supervision'	-	2
'minor'	3	1
Psychiatric treatment only:		
in-patient	1	1
Both criminal and psychiatric:		
'custodial' and in-patient	4	-
'supervision' and in-patient	2	-
No record of either:	4	5
Total	23	10

Table 5.10 lists all males and females who have been in institutional care according to whether they have a record of criminal sentences, or psychiatric treatment, or a combination of both.   It also discriminates according to the most serious type of criminal sentence received.

Of the twenty-three males experiencing care, fifteen (65 per cent) subsequently received 'custodial' and/or 'supervision' sentences.   Of these fifteen, six had also been in psychiatric hospital.   Three out of the ten females in care had received such sentences;   a further one had been in hospital.   Only four (17 per cent) males had neither a criminal record nor received psychiatric treatment, compared with five females (50 per cent).

Further overlaps concern other subjects in addition to those who have been in care.   Of the fourteen males who received psychiatric treatment, eight had received 'custodial' sentences, four 'supervision' sentences and one a 'minor' sentence.   The remaining male was fifteen and absconding from a community home.   Seven of these fourteen had been in care.   Of the five females who had treatment, only one, an out-patient, had a criminal record (probation);   and only one had been in care.   Of the thirty-one males who had received 'custodial' and/or 'supervision' sentences, twelve had had psychiatric treatment and fifteen had been in care.

Fifty per cent of our male sample and 34 per cent of the females have spent time in at least one 'institution' - defined here to include prisons, detention centres, borstals, psychiatric hospitals, community homes or equivalents.   Excluding those seven males and eight females whose only institutional experience was when in community homes, 40 per cent of the males and 11 per cent of the females have been in institutions specifically designed to contain or care for 'deviant' individuals.

ALCOHOL AND DRUGS

TABLE 5.11 Self-acknowledged difficulties arising from alcohol consumption

	Males	Females
Self-acknowledged difficulties in last six months	13	2

	Males	Females
Self-acknowledged difficulties longer ago than last six months	5	-
Total	18	2

We listed only those acknowledging that alcohol consumption had created a difficulty for them.   Most of those seeing it as a recent difficulty also saw possible problems in the future.   Those seeing it as a less recent problem felt it was over:

'It stopped me drinking.   I don't drink now nearly half as much as I used to ... I can drink two or three pints instead of drinking until I'm drunk.' (nineteen-year-old male talking about psychiatric treatment)

'I'm a trouble-maker with drink inside me ... I can't stop ... I started drinking heavily last year ... every night for two weeks ... I've cut down.   I only have one drink a night ... I start throwing punches when I'm drunk, but I can't fight.' (eighteen-year-old male)

'I suppose I was drinking a lot.   It led to me trying to kill myself....   The doctor told me I was an alcoholic.' (twenty-four-year-old female)

TABLE 5.12   Nature of main acknowledged difficulty (due to alcohol consumption)

	Males	Females
Tendency to violence	9	-
Tendency to non-violent crime	3	-
Aggravating unpleasant emotional state (e.g. suicidal tendencies)	4	1
'Too much' (excess)	1	1
Stomach ulcer	1	-
Total	18	2

Other subjects seemed to have a drink problem, but this view of ours was not shared.   One male had five convictions for drunkenness:

'I get drunk as often as I've got the money.   It's not a problem - if I haven't got the money, it doesn't bother me.'

Altogether, nine males had drunkenness convictions but
four, including the one above, do not appear in our table
because they saw drinking as creating no problems for
them.

   Whereas most of our subjects seemed partial to alcohol
and often consumed what seemed to us large quantities, the
regular use of 'drugs' was limited to a smallish minority.
Most were not interested and for some the word 'drugs' had
highly negative connotations.

   'I'm not interested - I get my kicks from fags and
   alcohol.' (male)

   'I'm not daft.' (female)

   'I've never been on drugs and never will.' (male)

   'I've had a pull at a smoke (cannabis) ... it's never
   interested me.' (male)

   Table 5.13 gives a rough-and-ready summary of 'drug'
use.   It distinguishes between 'current' (or recent)
users and those who see themselves as ex-users; and between 'regular' users (those who actively seek out sup-
plies) and 'occasional' users (those who take them when
offered by others).   The table assumes a ranking of
'drugs' in terms of 'hardness'.   Those listed as using
drugs in the upper categories may have (and usually had)
used drugs in the lower ones.   However the reverse does
not apply.   For instance, those classified as using
amphetamines/barbiturates had not used narcotics but may

TABLE 5.13   Use of psychotropic drugs

	Current/recent users		Ex-users	
	Regular	Occasional	Regular	Occasional
Narcotics	2 males		1 male	1 male
Amphetamines and/or barbiturates	6 males 1 female	3 males 1 female	2 males 1 female	2 males
LSD	2 males	3 males 2 females	2 males	1 male
Cannabis only	4 males 4 females	1 male	-	-
Total	14 males 5 females	7 males 3 females	5 males 1 female	4 males

have taken LSD and cannabis.   Some of those listed as ex-
users were also current users of less 'hard' drugs, but
they have not been listed twice.

Few saw drug-taking as being a problem.   Only two
males in the current regular narcotics category, two males
in the amphetamine category (one regular and the other
occasional) and two males in the LSD category (one current
and one past) identified drug usage as being a difficulty
or creating difficulties.   One reported:

> 'I had a bummer (LSD trip) about 18 months ago and I
> still get heavy flashbacks and feelings of fear.   I'm
> not sure I've come down yet.   I dropped about eight
> tabs, came on really heavy, had a total hallucination.
> A nazi guy jumped out of the wall, screaming, every
> part of me was scared, from the tips of my toes to the
> ends of my hair.   I thought I was dying.' (twenty-one-
> year-old male)

In only two cases did subjects show signs of drug
dependency.   One male had recently been in psychiatric
hospital for a drug 'cure' because he was on large dosages
of amphetamines.   Another male had been a registered
heroin addict for three years prior to our initial interview with him:

> 'I got into 'H' [heroin] at school.   I was just
> curious to start with.   Then I got addicted and became
> registered ... I've got no veins left now, I can only
> pop it [subcutaneous fix].'

Of the eighteen males and two females who acknowledged
that drinking had created problems, four males and one
female were still regular users of amphetamines/barbit-
urates and one female an ex-regular user.   One male
was still a regular user of LSD and another an ex-occa-
sional user.   Two males were regular current users of
cannabis.

ATTEMPTED SUICIDES

Eight males and six females claimed to have attempted to
kill themselves or endangered their lives as a means of
gaining help or attention.   Of these three males and
three females had had no psychiatric treatment.   The
usual methods were overdoses (eight subjects) and wrist-
slashing (four subjects).

We suspect that at least one female invented her

suicide attempt for melodramatic effect. One female said
she did it to get into hospital and one male, unsure about
his motives, felt that this may have been a motivation.

MISCELLANEOUS DISABILITIES

Our survey discovered two male epileptics (one was the
registered heroin addict). A further male was an enuretic who was thrown out of a Salvation Army hostel for
wetting the bed. One subject described himself as an
'asthmatic', although according to his probation officer
he exaggerated the extent of his disability to obtain
money and sympathy.
    Other handicaps included a male with a 'hole in the
heart'; two others from Glasgow damaged in various gang
fights (slashes and stab marks); another with a considerable speech impediment; and one partially blind in one
eye and deaf in one ear.

PREVIOUS HOMELESSNESS

Table 5.14 shows the extent of the sample's experience of
homelessness before their present stay in London. A
'homeless experience' is defined (rather more narrowly
than elsewhere) as one of sleeping rough for more than one
night in succession or staying in government reception
centres, lodging houses or night shelters.

TABLE 5.14 Aggregate length of previous 'homeless
experience'

	Males	Females
No previous experience	40	18
Under one month	18	14
One to six months	7	3
Over six months	7	-
Total	72	35

For seven males, homelessness had been a life-style for a
considerable part of their lives, usually intermittent and
interspersed with spells in institutions and/or more
settled accommodation. Five had been in community homes,
four had received psychiatric treatment (three as in-
patients) and all but one had criminal records (four 'custodial' and two 'supervision' only). Their ages ranged
between eighteen and twenty-two.

'I've been homeless on and off for years (since seventeen).' (male, aged twenty-one)

Altogether twenty males and six females had been homeless
in London on a previous occasion.

MARITAL TIES AND OFFSPRING

TABLE 5.15   Marital ties

	Males	Females
Married and accompanied by spouse to London	2	3
Married but permanently separated	7	1
Widowed	1	-
Married and temporarily separated	1	-
Total	11	4

A further three males and ten females arrived with a
partner but were not married to each other.   Of these two
young females claimed to be married but were almost certainly lying.

Five males who were married but permanently separated
have surviving offspring from their broken marriages.   A
further five males and two females not listed in the table
have offspring.   One male who owed maintenance arrears
was worried that he might be put in prison on this score.

Four females were between three and four months pregnant at the time of leaving for London.   Two of these
were anxious that their vagrant life would harm the baby:

'Where am I going to sleep?...   Am I going to lose the
baby?...   Just worried sick about losing the child.'

EDUCATION, WORK RECORDS AND QUALIFICATIONS

The table below gives a breakdown of our sample by the age
they left full-time education.   Sixty-four per cent of
the males and 46 per cent of the females left full-time
education at fifteen or before.   In addition, 11 per cent
of the males and 28 per cent of the females left as soon
as they were eligible to do so - this being after the
minimum leaving age had been raised to sixteen.   Four
males and two females went to ESN schools.

TABLE 5.16   Age of leaving full-time education

	Males	Females
15 or before	46	16
16 (minimum age allowed by law)	8	10
16 (over minimum age)	11	3
17-18	3	1
19-21	-	2
Officially not eligible to leave	2	3
False/unreliable data	2	-
Total	72	35

Table 5.17 below shows the highest qualifications our subjects obtained while in full-time education. Twenty-two per cent of the males and 26 per cent of the females claimed to have at least one CSE, 'O' level, 'A' level or their equivalents. However, we suspect at least a few were overstating or inventing their qualifications.

TABLE 5.17   Highest level of examination success while in full-time education

	Males	Females
Degree	-	1
'A' level or equivalent	3	2
'O' level or equivalent	8	2
CSE or equivalent	5	4
None	56	26
Total	72	35

One female about to set off on a world tour had a degree in Mathematics and another claimed to have finished Part I of a degree course before dropping out.

In addition, seven males claimed to have obtained various parts of City and Guild Certificates while serving apprenticeships; three of these their Part I, two their Part II, one his Part III and the other all parts.

The educational performance of our sample reflected that their attendance and motivation at school was often well below par.

'I wasted my education, I didn't agree with the system ... I wanted to earn some money.' (male, aged eighteen)

The following comment comes from a seventeen-year-old male

who had left school at the earliest opportunity to work in
a bookie's shop, a job he left after only two weeks:

'I felt I just didn't fit in ... I couldn't be bothered
with exams, I didn't even turn up.'

Lack of qualifications poses a serious handicap to a
school-leaver looking for his first job and indeed subsequent jobs.   We detected a high degree of alienation from
the methods and structure of the educational system by our
sample, and this extended to a suspicion and hostility
directed towards career officers and statutory employment
agencies:

'They couldn't care less about you ... they just send
you out with a piece of paper in your hand, another
bloody unit ... the job's gone when you get there
anyway.'

This from an eighteen-year-old male who had worked only
twice for short periods in casual labour.
     Table 5.18 shows how much of their potential working
lives our subjects spent in employment.   This includes
any period of their lives after leaving school or college
apart from time spent in institutions.   The 'not applicable' category contains those subjects whose potential
working lives had been less than six months.

TABLE 5.18   Percentage of potential working life employed

	Males	Females
75%-100%	11	4
50%-75%	19	9
25%-50%	24	10
0%-25%	14	6
Not applicable	4	6
Total	72	35

     If we exclude the 'not applicable' category, 56 per
cent of the males and 55 per cent of the females had been
unemployed for at least half their potential working
lives.   However, the table does not allow for the wide
variation in the lengths of time our subjects were eligible for employment.   In the case of the younger subjects this was often insufficient to warrant an assessment
of their work record since they had had little chance to
establish a particular pattern.   In addition, this (and

the following) information is liable to be particularly
unreliable.   It was difficult to elicit exact details
from our subjects.   The older ones especially had often
had many jobs and could not recall clearly their durations
or even how many they had had.   They did not think in
terms of 'curricula vitae' and their jobs were usually of
insufficient duration or not valued enough to be memor-
able.   Subjects tended to overstate their periods in employment (often unwittingly), although others probably
forgot to mention all the jobs they had had.

   Most of our subjects had only done unskilled types of
work, frequently on a short-term, casual basis.   Relatively few had certificates or experience that would
qualify them for skilled or even semi-skilled jobs.
Seven males claimed to have obtained City and Guild certificates to various levels.   Only two of these finished
their apprenticeships and had been working in skilled
occupations in manufacturing.   The other five had worked
as trainees in manufacturing and service industries but
would not be classed as skilled workers.   Of the other
males, only three had at some time done work that was not
unskilled;   this was clerical work, but their jobs had
been of short duration.   Of the females, only one had
done clerical work, and eight had worked as shop assistants.   The work experience of the rest of the sample
(sixty-two males and twenty-six females) was either restricted to unskilled work (mainly in the catering and
construction industries) or, in a few cases, was non-
existent.

   The turnover of jobs experienced by our sample was
high.   If we exclude the 'not applicable' category, the
average number of job starts for the males was 5.1 and
for the females 3.5.   Here we must remember that the
potential working lives of many of our subjects were
relatively short either because they had only recently
left school or because they had subsequently spent a con
siderable proportion of their lives in custodial or psychiatric institutions.   Job satisfaction in general was
low, perhaps a reflection of the types of jobs they were
doing.   Most jobs (63 per cent) were given up voluntarily.   The rest were lost as a result of disciplinary
action (23 per cent), redundancy (7 per cent), or not
being available for work - getting arrested, sickness
etc. (7 per cent).   Jobs were left, often on impulse,
because of dissatisfaction with pay, work-mates, bosses or
the arduous/routine nature of the work itself.   These
reasons were often combined with a desire for a change or
rest, or a general dissatisfaction with a working existence and other aspects of their lives.   Thirteen per

cent of all job leavings followed an argument with a
'boss'.

Our sample, with a few exceptions, were, by the time we
interviewed them, in the habit of either changing jobs
frequently or spending long periods unemployed.   Apart
from ten males and nine females, they only had experience
of unskilled work.   They had low expectations in the employment world and getting a job in London seemed more a
response to agency pressure than to any burning ambitions
to get jobs.   We asked our sample what jobs they expected
to find in London: 58 per cent of the males and 69 per
cent of the females replied that they would be happy with
living-in and kitchen portering jobs.   The remainder of
the sample were looking for other casual work: such as
builders' labourers, shop assistants, and warehousemen.
The difficulties of, first, obtaining work, and then being
able to keep it, daunted many:

'I can't get a job looking like this.'

'I haven't got the fare even to go to the interview.'

were typical comments.

Our sample seemed to be at the bottom of the labour
market.   Where jobs even for moderately well-qualified
young people are hard to get, interesting and fulfilling
work for young people who are less educated, less able to
compete in terms of appearance, often without the stability and support of a family network, and in unsettled
accommodation, is virtually unobtainable.

WHERE OUR SUBJECTS CAME FROM

Table 5.19 classifies each subject according to the region
or country where he last stayed for a near-continuous
period of at least one year.

Scotland tops the ranking order by a wide margin,
followed by the South East and North West.   The three
northernmost English regions together provided 26 per
cent of the males and 29 per cent of the females.
Ireland (both North and South) provided 17 per cent of
males but only 3 per cent of females.   The majority of
our subjects came from regions outside a radius of 200
miles from Charing Cross - roughly 68 per cent of males
and 52 per cent of females.

TABLE 5.19   Region or country* where last stayed a year or more

'Standard region' or country	Males	Females
Scotland	18 (25%)	7 (20%)
South East England (excluding GLC area)	9 (12½%)	5 (14%)
North West England	8 (11%)	6 (17%)
Eire	7 (10%)	1 (3%)
Yorks and Humberside	6 (8%)	3 (9%)
South West England	5 (7%)	2 (6%)
Northern England	5 (7%)	1 (3%)
Northern Ireland	5 (7%)	-
West Midlands	3 (4%)	4 (11%)
East Midlands	3 (4%)	2 (6%)
Wales	1 (1½%)	2 (6%)
Channel Islands	1 (1½%)	-
East Anglia	-	1 (3%)
Foreign: United States	1 (1½%)	-
France	-	1 (3%)
Total	72	35

* Using British Standard Regions as at April 1974.

In most cases, the region where our subjects last stayed one year or more was also the region where subjects were born and brought up. Eleven males and three females were exceptions.   If the table was based on birthplace, then the proportion of Scottish males would be even higher - 29 per cent instead of 25 per cent; Welsh males would be 4 per cent instead of 1½ per cent.

These percentages take no account of the relative sizes of regional populations.   Twice as many males in our population came from Scotland as from the South East. However, Scotland's population (5.2 million in 1974) is just over half that of the South East excluding the GLC area (9.8 million).   Relative to population size, Scotland provided our sample with nearly four times as many males as the South East.

We have calculated an index of propensity.   This index represents the ratio of the actual sample proportions coming from each region to the proportion to be expected simply on the basis of the region's population size. Scots provide 25 per cent of our male sample but Scotland only accounts for about 10 per cent of the population of the British Isles (which for our purposes includes Eire). The 'propensity' for Scottish males is 2.4 meaning that

the probability of any young male Scot becoming eligible
for selection into our sample is 2.4 times greater than
the average for the British Isles. The propensity for
West Midlands males is 0.4 meaning that a young male from
there is six times less likely to fall within our target
population as one from Scotland.

Indexes of propensity are presented for males and
females separately on the two maps. As a check we have
calculated a parallel set of indexes based on regional
breakdowns of the much larger numbers of admissions to
Centrepoint in 1975. The Centrepoint index is given in
brackets. Their figures do not, however, distinguish
between Northern Ireland and Eire.

Proponents of the political model of homelessness often
support their thesis by referring to the disproportion-
ately high numbers of homeless young people coming from
areas of high unemployment, such as Scotland and Eire.
There is some correlation between regional propensity and
unemployment rates (1975 figures) in the case of males.
Northern England is a major exception having a higher unemployment rate than Scotland but a much lower propensity. The Scottish propensity cannot be accounted for
simply by unemployment percentages although it is possible
that some Scots come from pockets of very high unemployment. Traditional patterns of migration or housing and
social environment may be equally or more significant.

Distance from London seems significant. In fact,
geographical distance correlates more closely with propen-
sities than do regional unemployment rates. If someone
comes from Scotland and finds himself homeless in London,
he may be less likely to return home say than someone
coming from Kent or the West Midlands. He has invested
more in coming, and returning is correspondingly more difficult. The longer he stays, the more likely he is to
be selected into our sample.

Another possibility is that males from further regions
find it more difficult to get established in London.
This might reflect cultural and language difficulties.
We found it often difficult to understand Glaswegian subjects. Generally they might find it more difficult to
get jobs because they have fewer marketable skills and
educational qualifications. Young people in the Home
Counties are, in general, more highly qualified than those
in Northern England, Scotland and Ireland. Perhaps the
low propensity for Wales - an area of well above-average
unemployment - reflects its relatively high level of educational attainment.

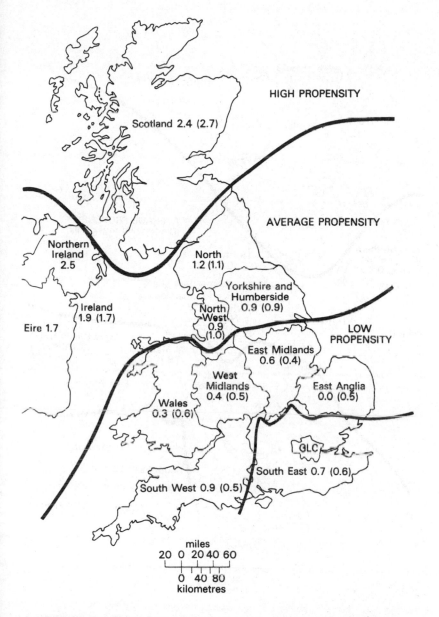

FIGURE 5.1 Index of propensity by region or country:
males (propensity based on Centrepoint population figures
for 1975 also given in brackets)

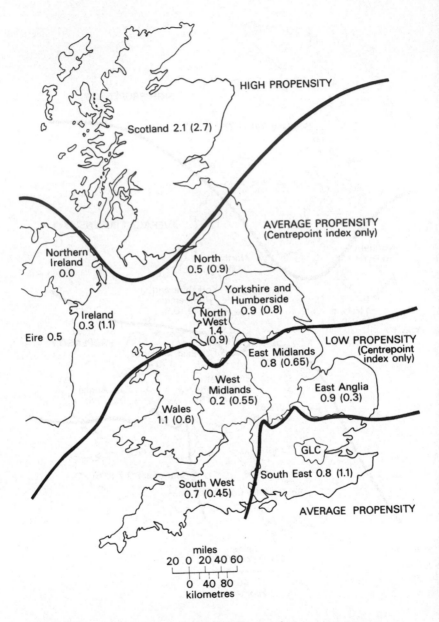

FIGURE 5.2   Index of propensity by region or country: females (propensity based on Centrepoint population figures for 1975 also given in brackets)

Chapter 6

MIGRATION
Why and how?

THE FORM OF MIGRATION

This chapter focuses on the why and how of our subjects'
migration to London. We approach this question from two
directions: why (and what) were they leaving and why did
they choose to come to London?

To take account of subjects who were geographically unsettled for a period before reaching London, we had to
choose a still point from which a subject could be said to
have left rather than simply 'moved on'. This we called
his 'last settled base' (LSB), defined arbitrarily as the
town or city in whose vicinity the subject has lived con-
tinuously for at least three months. In nearly all
cases, this was within the same region as given in our
regional analysis. We chose not to regard prison as a
last settled base.

As the tables show, fifty males and thirty females set
off intending to come to London. All came straight to
London except for four males and three females who stopped
briefly en route. The longest stop was two weeks by a
Dublin male who 'meant to come straight to London. Wales
seemed a good place, so I tried to get a job in the
hotels.' He illustrates how exploratory and open-ended
migration was for many.

TABLE 6.1 Destination intentions at time of setting out
from LSB

	Males	Females
To come to London	50	30
To go elsewhere	12	4
No LSB since leaving prison	7	-
Unreliable information	3	1
Total	72	35

TABLE 6.2   Length of time between leaving LSB and arriving in London

	Males	Females
Came straight to London	46	27
Within one week or less	7	4
One to two weeks	5	2
Two weeks to one month	1	-
One to two months	2	1
Two to three months	1	-
No LSB since leaving prison	7	-
Unreliable information	3	1
Total	72	35

Apart from the seven males with no LSB since leaving prison, twelve males and four females actually intended a destination other than London on setting off from their LSB.   They went to other places staying for periods of between one night and three months before coming to London.   For example, one male absconded from a community home and went to Luton staying for two weeks, first in a lodging house and then in a derelict house with an old Irishman.   He came on to London to be better 'hidden'. Another, jumping bail, went to stay with friends in Wales, but after two weeks came to London because 'I thought London would absorb me - make me more invisible'.   Another five males left their other destination because there was little work there.   The other five males and two of the females came on to London, mainly for a change of scene or because they wanted to keep moving.   The other two females re-directed themselves on hearing about the London homeless agencies.

Thirty-nine per cent of the males and 77 per cent of the females were accompanied on leaving their LSB.   While travelling to London, three males separated from their (male) travelling companions.   All seven males with no LSB since leaving prison arrived in London alone.

TABLE 6.3   Numbers leaving LSB accompanied

	Males	Females
With friend or acquaintance of same sex	20	12
As a couple (male and female)	5	13
With one platonic friend of the opposite sex	3	1
With two or more (platonic) friends	-	1
Total	28	27

THE LEAVING SITUATION: ACCOMMODATION AND EMPLOYMENT

Tables 6.4 and 6.5 give our subjects' accommodation and
employment situations on deciding to leave their LSB.
Most had little to lose by leaving.   We discuss later the
extent to which employment or accommodation difficulties
prompted them to leave.

TABLE 6.4   Occupation when deciding to leave LSB

	Males	Females
Unemployed	45	20
In work	13	9
At school	1	5
At technical college	1	-
In community home	2	-
No LSB since leaving prison	7	-
Unreliable information	3	1
Total	72	35

TABLE 6.5   Accommodation when deciding to leave LSB

	Males	Females
Living with parent(s)	29	11
Living with grandparent(s)	2	2
Living with parent(s) of boy/girl friend or spouse	1	1
In own or shared rented accommodation	14	10
In lodgings	2	-
Living in friends' accommodation	-	3
Living in job	-	2
Probation hostel	2	1
Mother and baby home	-	1
Psychiatric hospital	1	1
Community home	2	-
Homeless (including on the streets, homeless agencies, lodging houses, crash pad)	9	2
No LSB since leaving prison	7	-
Unreliable information	3	1
Total	72	35

MANNER OF LEAVING

The dominant pattern seemed one of snap decisions to leave
- in response to some perceived crisis or impulse - and
then departing almost immediately, allowing little time
for preparation or second thoughts.

'It was purely on impulse ... it was stupid of me to be
so impulsive.' (male)

'I just left without planning it.' (female)

'It was raining that afternoon so we just decided to
come up here.' (female from Kent)

Even when the idea was premeditated, there seemed
little preparation.

'We decided to come a month ago.   We were going to
save up but we got fed up with our jobs, gave a week's
notice and just came.' (female)

Very few gave leaving considerable attention:

'I thought about it and thought about it.' (male)

One telling index of their unpreparedness was the proportion arriving in London with less than £5:   53 per cent
of the males and 63 per cent of the females (see next
chapter).   In several cases lack of money was actually
given as a reason for leaving.
For many, leaving meant a step into the unknown - a
prospect tinged with adventure or release.   There was
commonly the feeling that you had to go and see for yourself and sometimes even that expectations were pointless.

'I never imagined it [London] to be anything.   I just
take things as they come.' (male)

In making the decision to leave they did not usually give
much attention to the difficulties they might face on
arrival.

'I never thought of the problems - I just wanted to get
out of Birmingham.' (female)

There was a strong tendency to believe that any difficulties could be transcended and what was to happen was
more a matter of 'fate' or 'luck' than within their power
to predict or control.

'[I thought] I'd try my luck.' (male)

'I just see how it goes, which way life goes, I just
let it come.' (male)

   Many left on an exploratory basis, knowing they could
return (for instance, resume living with parents). Most
felt that they were leaving a nothing-to-stay-for or at
least nothing-to-lose situation, although after arrival
they often soon began to appreciate and miss people and
things previously taken for granted: friends, home comforts, a familiar environment. Quite a few knew or
guessed that the agencies provided a safety net.

'I knew about these places - shelters and the like.'
(female)

MAIN REASONS FOR LEAVING LAST SETTLED BASE

Our subjects usually gave several reasons for leaving.
To simplify, we have typified our subjects by what we in-
ferred to be their main reason for leaving.

TABLE 6.6 Typification by main reason for leaving LSB

	Males	Females
Employment situation	14	6
Accommodation situation	11	0
Change of scene I (strong 'pull' element)	12	9
Change of scene II (predominant desire to get away)	11	3
Legal situation	8	-
Getting away from violent situations	4	-
Interpersonal problems	1	5
To accompany a friend of partner	-	3
Other (to score opium)	1	-
No LSB since leaving prison	7	-
Highly unreliable data	3	1
Total	72	35

   We did not base our inferences simply on what we were
told, because some subjects gave false or incomplete information. This occasionally led us to overrule their
stated reasons, as for instance in the case of a young

male who did not tell us he was absconding from a community home.

Our judgment also played an important role where subjects were inconsistent or uncertain about their main motivations or were unable or unwilling to express them. Their emphasis might shift from one reason to another. They might initially give one reason - perhaps a 'package' like 'to find work' or 'for a change' - but on probing we might uncover a more fundamental issue.   Such inconsistency did not necessarily imply that they were trying to mislead us.

The initial replies of a few subjects - 'I don't know really ... it was purely on impulse' - led us to question whether the whole notion of 'reason' was always relevant. At least several subjects seemed to respond to a general feeling or a jumble or stimuli and impressions rather than a 'reasoned' decision to leave.   Most subjects seemed more intent on acting than on reflecting, so that they failed to form or retain a clear picture of their decision-making.   Perhaps some only came to formulate their 'reasons' retrospectively.

We often demanded consistency from subjects not fully appreciating that their 'reasons' were reconstructions continually to be revised as the perspective changed. One failing of our typification is that it reflects inadequately the inconsistency and uncertainty shown by many subjects and the role we played in eliciting their 'reasons'.

We looked at reasons for leaving their LSB (and for coming to London) in terms of 'push' and 'pull'.   Usually both the dominant 'push' and 'pull' seemed on the same dimension;   for instance: being unemployed (as main 'push') - more jobs in London (as main 'pull') or being 'bored' - desire for a change of scene.   There were exceptions;   for instance: accommodation difficulties (main 'push') - desire for a change (main 'pull').

Whereas their migration could be explained from two standpoints - reasons for leaving LSB or coming to London - we chose the former as our baseline question, partly because it seemed more fundamental.   The 'push' in the leaving situation outweighed the 'pull' in most cases.   Even where the 'pull' seemed strong - in 'change of scene' and to some extent in the 'employment' and 'accommodation' categories - it was often preceded by a strong 'push' element.   Usually, however, the main reason for coming to London either coincided with or was implicit in the main reason for leaving.

We hope the typification that follows reflects the wide diversity in the situations our subjects left, their

reasons for leaving and their orientations in coming to
London.

Employment situation (as main reason for leaving)

This category contains fourteen males and six females.
All males were unemployed at the time of leaving.   Seven
had been unemployed for up to a month and five for four
months or more.   Four females were unemployed.   The
other two had jobs which they gave up to come to London,
one on the mistaken assumption that she had a living-in
job there.
Two subjects expressed a general theme:

'There's not a lot of work (in the Western Isles of
Scotland).   The only work there is on the oil rigs and
I don't fancy that.' (male, aged nineteen)

'I decided there's no future in Dublin for me.   I'll
go over to London and see what's there.' (male, aged
twenty)

Regionally the majority of the males (eleven out of
fourteen) came from areas of severe unemployment: Northern Ireland (1), Eire (4), North-West England (3) and
Scotland (3).   Both males and females assumed there
would be well-paid jobs in London.   Most wanted unskilled or semi-skilled jobs and were not particularly
selective.   Only one subject had a job to come to: a
living-in job which he lost after six weeks.   One female
came to take a six-week course as a computer punch card
operator, but ran out of money.
They varied considerably in the strength of their commitment to work.   For a few employment seemed by far the
main motive in leaving

'There was no jobs at home ... I didn't leave because I
wanted to.   I had to.' (male, aged eighteen, from
Eire)

However, most subjects in this category also seemed
moved by a desire for adventure, change and enhancing
their social lives:

'[I thought] I'm going to a great place, a great job, a
big city.' (female, aged twenty-one)

It was particularly difficult to decide whom to include

in this category.   The large majority of our subjects referred to the desire for a job or a better job when giving
reasons for leaving or for choosing London.   In classify-
ing our subjects, we had to decide whether or not it was
their main reason for departing.   Frequently, the employment motivation seemed weaker than a desire for a change
of scene or accommodation difficulties.   For instance we
classified this male (from rural Eire) under 'Change of
scene I':

> 'I've come for work.   Well, I had a job where I lived
> but you want to see something new.   You get cheesed
> off with the social life in the town - there's nothing
> in it.   There's only one dance hall and that's very
> young, I mean twelve to thirteen-year-olds ... it hap-
> pens to everyone at a certain age.   You get browned
> off in the country.   You want to work in other places
> for the experience - it'll harden you up....'

Sometimes being unemployed seemed significant less as a
'push' and more as a void, a nothing-to-stay-for or no
ties situation.   As one male - generally 'fed up' for a
host of reasons - remarked:

> 'I wasn't working or anything.'

Subjects frequently overstated their work orientation,
perhaps with an eye to the expectations of the agencies.
One male initially gave his reason as 'to find work'.
When probed, he admitted there was 'plenty' of work in his
home town (Leicester) and then amended his reason - rather
playfully - to 'a change, to see the sights'.

Accommodation situation

This category contains eleven males and eight females.
Five of these males decided to leave mainly as a result of
having recently become homeless.   Two were locked out of
their parental home as a result of a conflict;   two were
evicted from their flat or lodgings when unable to pay
their rent;   and one was evicted from a squat.

> 'I got a £10 a week giro and the rent was £7 - I
> couldn't do it ... once you're on the streets you've
> got no chance.' (male, aged twenty-one)

Four males and seven females, living with their
parents, decided to leave mainly because of actual or

anticipated conflict with parents.   These males were aged
between eighteen and twenty-two, and the females between
fifteen and eighteen (with the exception of one, aged
twenty-four).

'My father was impossible ... he was narrow-minded ...
conservative ... he left me to do all the cooking and
washing up.' (his mother had died) (male, aged nineteen)

'I'm a bit of a wild one.   They [her parents] say they
want to put me in a home ... they say I'm out of control ... it's my father's fault....   You won't tell
them, will you?   I don't want to go home.' (female,
aged fifteen, running away from home)

The remaining female, aged nineteen, left, not because
of conflict but to secure independent accommodation:

'There's no chance [of accommodation] in Wrexham.   All
you do is sign on the housing list and you have to wait
five years.'

The remaining males (two) were in other accommodation.
One was living with his fiancée's parents and left because
of friction.   The other, living at a probation hostel,
left after losing his job because of drunkenness, probably
because he was too ashamed to face the hostel staff:

'I came to London because I knew I could get a bed
here.'

Accommodation difficulties usually seemed insufficient
to explain why they left their LSB (rather than seeking
more acceptable accommodation there).   Only four males
and one female left because they anticipated better accommodation in London.   The female wanted a flat; the four
males intended to stay at the homeless agencies (where
three had stayed before).   Four girls aged between fifteen and seventeen saw themselves as 'running away from
home':

'[London] It's the place you make for when you're running away - it's big, you can get lost in it.'

The remaining subjects were pulled by better employment
prospects and/or a desire for a change of scene:

'I wanted to go anyway ... I wanted a change - to

brighten my life up a bit ... to get away from Liverpool.' (male, aged twenty-one, recently kicked out by
his step-father)

Change of scene I (strong 'pull' element)

For subjects in both this and the next category, their
main reason for leaving was the desire for a change of
scene.   We have placed here those defining their migration in terms of 'pull' - the forward-looking desire to
experience another place.   The next category contains
those whose emphasis is almost exclusively on getting away
from their LSB.

This category contains twelve males and nine females.
Most were 'pulled' by the desire for 'a change' and also
by the specific attractions of London - the 'sights',
'bright lights', amusement arcades, 'night life', its
size and 'pace'.   Three males and two females however set
off from their LSB with the intention of going somewhere
else.

Their emphasis varied between a tourist/travel orientation and a social life/leisure one, although usually both
were implied:

'I want to see some new faces and visit new places.'
(male)

For those who had not seen London before, there was
often curiosity:

'I wanted to see what it's really like.' (male)

Sometimes there was a strong 'push' as well as strong
'pull' element:

'We were bored - there was nothing there - no work, no
nightclubs, it was dead ... I always wanted to come to
London.   Everyone who'd been to London said it was
good.' (female, aged seventeen)

For seven males and one female, coming to London was
linked with more extensive travel ambitions.   The female
was in London to pick up visas for a world tour with her
husband.   One male, aged seventeen, was resuming a life-
style of travelling that he began at fifteen:

'I go round seeing towns.   I go there to see what
they're like....   What is there to settle down for?
I like to keep moving.'

For the other six males, London was the first step in
their travel programme:

> 'I wanted the best of both worlds - to come over here
> [from Eire] and see and do a lot, without doing too
> much work ... earn some bread, go to Morocco for the
> winter ... a chance to go somewhere else and meet
> people ... make the most of London, see some bands....'
> (male, aged twenty-one)

Of remaining subjects, most came to London on an exploratory, even 'tourist' basis.   Only two seemed defi-
nitely committed to staying long term: 'a new start' (the
female) and 'to expand, branch out a bit' (the male).
All but two (both females) mentioned coming to London
to find work.   However, this often seemed more of an intention - a means of supporting themselves whilst enjoying
London - than a reason for leaving their LSB.

Change of scene II (predominant desire to get away)

This category contains eleven males and three females.
They had a powerful, sometimes desperate, desire to get
away linked with a feeling of disenchantment, of being
'bored', 'fed up', 'sick', 'depressed' or 'a bit sorry for
myself':

> 'I came because I was sick ... I just wanted to get
> away ... I wanted a break.' (male, aged twenty-three)

This feeling could not be associated with any particular aspect of the situation.   It seemed to have several
associations.   One male could not even find a reason for
being 'fed up'.   Three males had recently broken up with
their wives.   Another male's wife had died eight months
previously in a car accident.   However, for these four
other factors such as no money, no job or no friends also
contributed to 'fed-upness':

> 'I was fed up.   Everything was happening.   I wasn't
> working or anything.   I separated from my wife.   I
> told her to get out.   It was after that I decided to
> come.   I wanted to make a clean break.'

Another male left his wife and two children to 'escape
myself and my responsibilities'.   Two other males and two
females were disillusioned with their life in their home
town:

'I was fed up there [Glasgow] - there was nothing much
to do, the place is dead ... I didn't like where I was
working.... It's too dangerous, too many gangs ... I
wanted to see life in London - to see if it's any
good.' (male, aged seventeen)

The remaining female (aged sixteen) had experienced
serious conflict with her parents and at school and had
been in a young people's psychiatric unit. She had then
been expelled from school just before taking 'O' levels.

The three remaining males expressed persistent feelings
of unhappiness which were not of recent origin. Two
gratuitously related the feeling to a long history of both
rejection and persecution by relatives or acquaintances
and by the various officials involved in putting and keeping them in custodial and psychiatric institutions:

'I blame my brother - if he had helped me after what I
went through and suffered and after my father died, I
would never have touched London.' (male, aged twenty,
referring to when he was sixteen)

'They've picked on me since I was twelve.... They
[officials and acquaintances] want to make me cry
again ... I can't stand it any more ... I want to sort
out the present. If it doesn't work out in London,
where will it work out?' (male, aged twenty-three)

Legal situation

All but one of the eight males in this category were leaving to get away from a legally binding situation: court
order (2), mental health section (1), bail (3) and probation order (1). They had become fugitives.

Three were absconding, two (aged fifteen and sixteen)
from community homes and one from a Scottish psychiatric
hospital. One (aged fifteen) later told us:

'I gave you slightly false information in case I was
tracked ... I don't think I need care. I'm quite
happy on my own ... I think being homeless in London is
the only alternative.'

Three were jumping bail, although only one admitted
this. He told us he was 'frightened of being put in
prison' on a drugs charge because of previous convictions.
A further two males and one female were on bail in their
LSB. They are not included here because they left primarily for other reasons.

Another male, aged twenty, left the probation hostel where he lived as a condition of a probation order:

> 'I'm tired of people telling you what to do - proba-
> tion officers, hostels.   Come in, do this and do that.
> It gets on your nerves.   You've been inside [borstal]
> and somebody else starts and does it.'

He was very anxious because he owed rent and £90 maintenance arrears for his illegitimate child.
The remaining male was running away from the police:

> 'I had a rough time in Scotland getting jailed all the
> time ... I left 'cos I kept getting in trouble ... the
> police get on your back and hassle you.'

Given the number of false names and/or addresses, we
suspect that several other subjects might be eligible for
this category.

Getting away from violent situations

This category contains four males.   Two were fleeing
reprisals from teenage gangs.   One, aged eighteen, had
been in a Dublin skin head gang:

> 'A couple of people were after me ... I cut someone's
> head with a bottle.'

The other, aged nineteen, was a Glasgow gang leader.
His body bore testimony to frequent slashes and stabs.
He wanted to reform and escape the violence in Glasgow.
The remaining two were from Northern Ireland, and left
primarily to avoid sectarian strife.   One had harboured
two men in trouble with a paramilitary faction and so was
now in trouble himself.   The other, a Catholic travelling
with a Protestant friend, said:

> 'I left to get away from the troubles ... you can't go
> out at night ... innocent people getting killed ... you
> have to watch yourself and who you're with.'

Interpersonal problems

This category (which excludes those with parental problems) contains one male and five females.   The male
wanted to get away from his mother-in-law who 'kept coming

round and interfering'.   Four females had problems with
boyfriends.   For example:

> 'If he wants me he can come and get me - I did it to
> teach him a lesson.'

The remaining female had just had her baby adopted which
led to her friends turning on her:

> 'The aggravation made me leave.   People talking about
> the baby all the time.'

To accompany a friend or partner

This category contains three females.   One from France
was with her husband who was avoiding conscription into
the army.   Another was with her 'husband' looking for
work.   The other female had been sleeping rough in Birmingham with her boyfriend.   She was about to return home
when a group of friends, including her boyfriend, suggested that she accompany them to London:

> 'I didn't like the idea ... I wanted to go home to my
> mother ... I had to be persuaded - this girl said we'd
> all get a flat together [in London].'

There were several other cases where the suggestion of
a friend precipitated leaving.   We have not classified
them here because there seemed to be other, stronger,
reasons for their leaving than the desire to accompany the
friend.   Take for instance a girl who came to London at
the instigation of another girl:

> 'I didn't like Edinburgh ... I didn't know anywhere
> else to go ... I've always wanted to see London ...
> [but] I wouldn't have come on my own, 'cos I kenned no
> one [there].'

No settled base since leaving prison

This category comprises seven males.   They had been out
of prison from between two days and nine months before
arriving in London.   Two came straight to London after
being released.   Both felt - as one said:

> 'I've nothing to go home for.'

and chose London because they knew of homeless agencies
and squats there.   One was intent on having a 'good time'
in the West End.
    Another two males arrived in London about two weeks
after release.   Both were fugitives.   In his short time
out, one had 'done' a filling station and was hiding from
the police.   He said 'I've always had robbing in me.'
The other left his home town because his mother was trying
to get him put back in psychiatric hospital.
    Another male arrived in London several weeks after
serving an eighteen months' sentence for rape.   He came
to London 'to pick up a girl, steal a car, go to Brighton
and rape her.'   A further male out of prison for six
months had spent most of this time 'rambling and thieving'
in Eire, leaving for England after being arrested for burglary and thereby jumping bail.
    The remaining male had been out of prison nine months,
travelling around the country.   He slept rough, lived in
lodging houses and did casual labouring with periodic returns to his home town of Leeds.   He had decided to go
straight and settle down.

    'It's the first time I've wanted to settle down - I'm
    sick of the thumbing around bit ... having no money ...
    you can't tell lies to the SS all your life.'

Highly unreliable information

Three males and one female gave such extensively false
and/or highly unreliable information that we had no guide
to the nature of their LSB or reasons for leaving it.
All four seemed intent on creating false identities and
life-stories.
    Two males were accomplished liars.   One was pretending
to be dumb.   The other, who stressed his 'good references', listed a bogus career as an itinerant, skilled hotel
worker.   He was keen to present himself as carefree, in-
dustrious and law-abiding:

    'I enjoy travelling ... I enjoy working ... having
    money in my pocket, and the best way of getting money
    is to work for it.'

The other two subjects were highly inconsistent, implausible liars.   The male even let his real names slip
out.   His story involved a quick succession of deaths -
his father, his mother and then his aunt with whom he had
gone to live.   His aunt's lodger had promptly responded

by 'booting' him out.   He had the appearance of a fugitive and mentioned that he was afraid of being picked up
by the police for having 'no fixed abode'.   The female,
one of our 'tragic heroines', claimed she had been living
in a community home until the staff made her leave:

> 'It was either go to London or go home' [to her
> mother].

WHY CHOOSE LONDON?

Usually reasons for choosing London were implicit in their
reasons for leaving their LSB.   London was variously seen
as promising better job or accommodation opportunities;
a sanctuary from threatening or disturbing situations and/
or a change of scene, the freshness, excitement or challenge of a new, more diverse environment and the chance to
meet 'new people'.   In the large majority, the specific
attractions of London - the 'sights', 'bright lights', its
size and scope - exerted a 'pull', sometimes very powerful
especially among those who had not been before:

> 'I reckoned the capital of England has everything.'
> (male)

> 'We chose London because it was the biggest place.'
> (male)

Sometimes the known existence of homeless agencies provided an incentive:

> 'Being on the streets of Birmingham is no good -
> London has got projects you can use.' (male, homeless
> before leaving)

However, leaving usually seemed more a response to a
'push' than to the specific 'pull' of London.   It was
more a matter of wanting to leave and then deciding where
(and when) to go.   Because of its unique reputation and
attractions, London led other possible destinations:

> 'Like me, kids come to London for excitement and mainly
> because they are sick ... you want to get away and
> London is the only place that comes to mind.' (male in
> 'Change of scene II')

Excitement and curiosity was stimulated by London's
reputation, gleaned from the media and/or acquaintances
who had been:

'They call it the big smoke and they say it's really good.... It's always the first place you'd head for. ... When you read about London you hear the streets are paved with gold.' (male)

'People will always come to London - even if they have to sleep out, they will still come - they hear so many stories.'

There were sixteen males and four females who came with a highly idealised view of London and who, even by the initial interview were strongly disillusioned. Well-paid jobs and flats were much harder to find than expected. London was either 'just like anywhere else' or worse - 'the people are unfriendly', 'everyone is rushing around', 'it's a rat race', 'there are no bright lights or anything - it's one big expensive town'.

'I thought when I came to London my life would change. I'd heard all sorts of stories ... big fantastic place; all big flashing lights ... plenty of women, plenty of everything ... it's all a pack of lies.... It's just the same as anywhere else only it's a bigger place.' (male)

'I thought I'd get a flat straight away. I'd be made, that there was money flying around in all directions, but I've found it not so easy.' (male)

'Everything is on top of me. I'm frightened by the size of London. I've made no friends at all. I wouldn't have come here if I'd known what it was like.' (female, aged twenty-three)

At least a further sixteen males and six females had high and probably unrealistic expectations but had not yet been disappointed by the initial interview.

'It's fantastic only I want to see the sights ... I should get a job and a flat OK.' (male, on day of his arrival)

'It's been great - like on telly.' (female, second night in London)

These people, cushioned by the homeless agencies, were responding mainly as tourists. They had not yet tested the economic realities of finding work and accommodation. Their first impressions could be misleading as we found in the follow up.

The remainder came with lower expectations.   Usually they anticipated some difficulties, although most erred towards assuming that finding jobs and reasonable accommodation would be easier than experience taught.

'I knew it would be hard, but not this hard.' (male)

At least thirty-six males and seventeen females had been in London before - nineteen males and nine females within the last two years.   Of these, twenty males and six females were able to base expectations on previous experience of homelessness in London.   However veering towards optimism, they might also be disappointed as with the male saying:

'It was all right when I was here before.'

The remainder who had visited but had not been homeless had either once lived in London with their parents or had briefly visited on a holiday or trip.   Such an experience often seemed misleading as a guide to settling there. One male who had holidayed two years earlier said:

'It was good ... I was with a group of fellas ... I only saw the good things.'

Three males said they came with no expectations.   A further three males and three females were finding life in London better than expected.

'I'm doing fine now [promise of a place in a squat] - I didn't know what to expect.' (male)

'I told my wife we could be destitute for four weeks ... London's better than I thought - the wages are better ... you can get a living-in job ... it seems easy to get a job ... the city's all right - there are no fights.' (male from Glasgow)

'I had no delusions ... I knew it would be cold and hard ... there's more help here than I thought [e.g. Centrepoint] ... I expected to be dossing.' (female, aged sixteen)

However, the over-all tendency was towards eventual disillusionment.   This was often partial and less to do with London as a place and more with their standpoint of homelessness and destitution.

'London is a big place - it's hard to break into.'
(male)

'If you've got accommodation in London and plenty of
money it's great.   But if you've got nothing it's
terrible in London, worse than in Birmingham.'
(female, previously homeless in Birmingham)

Chapter 7

TIME IN LONDON

This chapter looks at subjects' experiences in London in
the period that extends up to twelve months after arrival.
(By arrival we refer to the one that occurred immediately
prior to the initial interview.)   We are mainly concerned
with the time they spent homeless in London.   Most subjects were interviewed soon after arrival: 57 per cent of
the males and 63 per cent of the females within their
first week in London.   This means that for much of the
time they spent in London our data is incomplete.   We
have had to rely on our follow-up sample, comprising
twenty-nine males and sixteen females.   This may not be
representative of our whole sample (see next chapter).

ARRIVAL AND GETTING TO THE PROJECTS OF INTERVIEW

Table 7.1 shows how they travelled to London.   The
'other' category includes one male who flew, one cycling
and another walking.   Some of those who hitched made the
rail or bus terminals their first port of call so as to
deposit luggage.

TABLE 7.1   Means of travel to London

	Males	Females
Hitching	34	17
Train	21	14
Bus	10	4
Other	3	-
Unknown	4	-
Total	72	35

Table 7.2 shows how much money they had on arrival.
Where friends came together they usually pooled resources;
we simply apportioned the pooled total.   The figures
given are unlikely to be reliable.   One tendency is to
overstate the amount of money brought to avoid accusa-
tions of improvidence.   This may be accompanied by the
standard hard luck story of their money being lost or
stolen.   Seven subjects gave this story.   In the case of
the male claiming to be 'dumb' it was certainly fabricated.   Three males listed with over £35 claimed to have
been robbed during the first few days.   Two males claimed
to have lost all their money on route.   One female
claimed that her own and her friend's money (£10 in total)
had been forcibly taken on the first day, by a man in a
squat.   On the other hand, there may have been a tendency
to understate the amount of money, either because they had
squandered it or because they still had some left.   A
condition imposed by the projects might be that they were
destitute.   WERC defined this rigidly as having less than

TABLE 7.2   Finances on arriving in London

	Males	Females
Less than £5	38	22
£5 up to £15	10	3
£15 up to £25	8	4
£25 up to £35	7	3
£35 or more	7	1
Unreliable data	1	-
No data	1	2
Total	72	35

£1.   A few subjects admitted that they had not declared
all their money to the project.   Others may have done the
same with us.

Fifty-three per cent of the males and 63 per cent of
the females had less than £5 on arrival.   Of these many
were destitute on arrival and the rest usually within one
or two days.   Those arriving with more money fared little
better.   Some openly admitted 'blowing' the money.   One
male brought £25 and in two days 'drank and ate it away'.
Another had £60 (for two) and spent it in three days
'swanning around in taxis'.   Most were unprepared for
London prices:

'It feels really bad having nowhere to go in the day.

We get put out at 8.00 in the morning (from Centrepoint).   What do you do?   Money goes on cups of
coffee....   We sat in Piccadilly Circus most of the
time ... it felt really bad.' (male)

Only two subjects had pre-arranged accommodation in
London.   One girl, coming for a short residential course,
had booked lodgings;   a male had arranged a living-in job.
A further male and female had been put up - for one night
only - by acquaintances met on previous visits to London.
A few others thought they had addresses to go to but found
their contacts had moved or were inhospitable.   Only
three males (including the one with the living-in job) had
pre-arranged jobs to come to.
The majority of the sample were new to London and homelessness and were confused and disorientated on arrival.
Travel was difficult and distances seemed great, especially for the destitute who walked everywhere:

'I have to walk everywhere because I've got no money.
The labour exchange sent me miles around for jobs when
I did not even know my way around London.' (male)

'I didn't know what to do.   I didn't know where to go
for a job so we were just wandering around looking at
the sights....   There seemed to be no factories or
building sites to go to try and get jobs.' (male)

'I come from a small village, I don't know towns.
It's very hard to meet people here, you feel really
lonely.   Everybody is rushing around.' (female)

Twenty males and six females had been homeless in
London before their present stay.   Some were well
acquainted with the homeless agencies and in several cases
were attracted to London by their presence:

'It's brilliant here [Centrepoint].   If someone's got
no money I tell them to come here.   Even if they have
got money I tell them to come here and keep quiet about
it.' (female)

Well over half the subjects reached the projects of
interview within one week of arriving in London.   Thirty-
nine per cent of the males and 51 per cent of the females
reached them before their third night in London.   Those
arriving with sufficient money had usually stayed in cheap
bed-and-breakfast or very basic 'hotel' accommodation
until their money had run out.   One male stayed one night

in an expensive hotel which made him destitute on his
second day.   A few subjects had stayed with casual contacts, usually for a day or two.   One female found a
place in a squat on her first day and stayed for five
weeks before it was pulled down.   Another stayed in a
cheap 'hotel' for six weeks, but she and her husband had
to leave when she lost her social security payment.   Not
knowing about the agencies, they wandered the streets for
several days until she collapsed with malnutrition and was
referred by the hospital to Centrepoint.

A minority of subjects had stayed at other agencies
before reaching the project of interview, but usually for
no longer than one or two nights.   These included Salvation Army hostels (where subjects were sometimes referred
by social security offices), Bit's crash pad, reception
centres and various night shelters and hostels.

Thirty-nine per cent of the males and 43 per cent of
the females slept rough before the initial interview.
This included sleeping or sheltering in stations, parks,
laundrettes, derelict houses, all-night cafés and various
street settings (for instance, the Charing Cross Arches).
It often meant simply walking the streets.   The longest
time anyone slept rough before the initial interview was
nearly three weeks.   This male spent the night time in
all-night cinemas and cafés, earning money by casual work
in the Covent Garden market.

Subjects usually slept rough either because it took
time to discover the agencies or because they were reluctant to use the agencies they were initially referred to
(in particular Salvation Army hostels).   Two young girls,
both running away from home, avoided the agencies rather
than run the risk of being returned home.   One slept
rough for two weeks before hunger drove her to Centrepoint.   The other eventually collapsed from malnutrition
and was briefly hospitalised, after which she sought help
from St Martins Social Services Unit (who she claimed did
inform the police):

> 'I stayed out for five days.   It gets a bit cold but
> if you've eaten something and had a drink it's all
> right.   You get used to it after a while - obviously
> you get cold but you just have to suffer it.'

A few subjects saw sleeping rough as having advantages,
as compared to staying at the agencies.   These included
companionship and lack of constraints:

> 'I'd rather sleep the streets than go into a cell, you
> get lonely ... if you go and join other people you're

OK.   It's quite good fun.   You talk to the old people
... they like you to talk to them and I was lonely.'
(male, seventeen years old)

Those few experienced at sleeping rough knew the best
places and prepared for it.   One male wore three layers
of outer clothing at the initial interview.   Another subject who was a skilled survivor spent three comfortable
nights in a funeral parlour.
     Table 7.3 shows how subjects heard about or were refer-
red to the project of interview.   Sometimes referrals
took the form of a chain as subjects were sent from one
agency to another until they reached the project.

TABLE 7.3 Source of referral to project of interview

Referral source	Project of interview				
		Male		Female	
	WERC	Centre-point	North	Centre-point	North
Grapevine (informal network)	9	12	2	10	–
Voluntary agencies	10	6	5	7	4
Penal and medical institutions	1	–	–	2	–
Self	5	6	–	4	–
Police	2	3	1	4	1
Social services	2	–	1	–	1
Social security offices	2	–	–	–	–
Other	1	1	–	2	–
Unknown	2	1	–	–	–
Total	34	29	9	29	6

The category of Voluntary agencies covers a wide spec-
trum, including, for example, St Martins, Blenheim Project, Soho Project, Irish Centre, The Samaritans and Bit.
North had closer connections with the alternative information agencies and the squatting grapevine - six out of the
fifteen referrals to North came from Bit who referred only
one to Centrepoint and none to WERC.   Bit was reluctant
to refer to Centrepoint because of the selection criteria
and limited length of stay.   They also found that their
clients were rarely accepted.   North had the advantage of
being in a squatting area which could mean longer-term

housing.   Many voluntary agencies made referrals to WERC
reluctantly and then only the older or more resilient
client.

One female who contacted the Samaritans was alarmed by
the nature of the questioning:

'They asked me all these questions, I put the phone
down, I didn't like it ... I didn't want them to help
me.'

We asked the subjects about seeking help.   Most were
unconcerned about seeking help from the projects.   Eleven
males and eight females expressed reluctance to ask for
help:

'I don't like it [asking for help] I've never asked for
it before.   I suppose there's got to come a time when
you do ask someone for help.'

'I've never been in one of these places before ... I
like to feel independent.   When you go to those places
you're not independent - you're hoping that they are
going to be nice enough and kind enough to let you in,
otherwise you're out, so you're dependent on someone
else and that isn't right.'

Sixteen (22 per cent) of the males and three females
(9 per cent) were ashamed of being homeless or destitute,
which was often linked with asking for help:

'I was in two minds whether to sleep in the park or the
street because it feels like sinking right down ...
I've always been fighting to stay above because of my
parents sinking right down ... I feel inadequate, I
can't take care of myself ... I've become someone I
despise.   When I see people asking for money in the
street I think there's no reason they need to be doing
that.   I always felt superior.   Now I'm down.   I'm
one of them.'

AT THE PROJECT OF INTERVIEW

Qualifying for help

On arrival at Centrepoint or WERC, subjects underwent an
induction procedure.   At Centrepoint this involved being
questioned at the gate, and further, fairly informal questioning (and counselling) inside usually after they had

eaten.   At WERC it involved having a shower (while their
clothes were searched for lice) and then answering a list
of questions.   It usually took a few days before subjects
saw a Resettlement Officer.

Especially at Centrepoint, subjects were confronted
with the problem of qualifying for admission and re-admission.   This sometimes led to their presenting themselves
in counterfeit or selective ways: for instance, under-
stating age or length of time homeless; giving a false
name (if they had previously been refused re-admission);
overstating their motivation and efforts to secure work
and more settled accommodation; and concealing less
acceptable reasons for being in London.

> 'Centrepoint's all right but it's a bit of a hassle to
> get in there, isn't it?   You have to start explaining
> where you've been and how old you are and you have to
> tell a couple of lies, do a bit of pattering here and a
> bit of pattering there.'

Self-packaging is a major response to the problems of
survival.   It may take the direction of appearing more
'normal' and provident than is the case.   Alternatively,
it may involve inventing or exploiting inadequacies and a
deprived background.   Our subjects tended to prefer the
former approach.

This strategy was not only used to qualify for resources but also to guard against intrusion and anticipated
recriminations.   This was more likely to apply at WERC
where questioning was more formal and usually felt to be
less than sympathetic.   For instance, one said he responded by 'telling them the first thing that comes into my
head - I don't want them to know my business'.   Another
male compared WERC's induction procedure to a 'concentration camp'.   He falsely claimed that he had no criminal
record, no dependents and no money on arrival:

> 'You have to give them all your particulars ... it's
> none of their business ... a waste of time....   If I'd
> told them about the money [£25], they'd have asked me
> what I'd done with it - and then you'd have another big
> inquest.'

What agencies called 'help' might sometimes be experienced by clients as pressure or intrusion or as merely
irrelevant.   This is illustrated by one female, aged sixteen, looking back on her stay at the GALS hostel and subsequent experiences:

'[The staff] got on my nerves, full of common sense and
what's good for you ... I was at the stage when I resented that - like teachers at school ... I was sent
home because they thought I was beginning to drift.
I didn't feel ready.   I wanted to stay two weeks more
but GALS thought I was a passenger living off the SS
[social security].'

She returned home to Edinburgh to an unsympathetic home
situation.   Her mother was 'fed up' with her and school
would not have her back.   She felt that life was
'futile', found an office job which was 'soul-destroying',
lasted a week, and returned to London.   She wanted to
'make a go of it' and see a boyfriend met on the previous
visit.   She could not find him, was not allowed in by
Centrepoint, went to a student hostel and took an overdose.

'I knew no one.   There was no chance of my going back
home.   They didn't welcome me ... I took the pills
because I was in London alone and had no one to turn
to, no one who cared.   I couldn't have done it in
Edinburgh because I knew people there.'

Subjects' evaluation of the projects of interview

The views presented below are in response to open-ended
questions about the project of interview - for instance,
'What do you think of WERC?'.   We tried not to provide
them with the dimensions on which they should evaluate the
project.   Some subjects made no specific evaluation,
saying, for instance, 'It's all right'.   Reference points
for evaluation varied.   Those who had been sleeping rough
put a high value on bed and warmth;   those who had stayed
in 'dirty' agencies such as the Salvation Army or Bit's
crash pad tended to note and value cleanliness;   those who
were lonely were concerned about personal contact.   Some
did not feel in a position to make a critical evaluation:

'You can't complain about these things; you're grateful
for a bed when you've been out all night.' (WERC male)

'What can you expect? it's all right for free.' (WERC
male)

Since the probability of a client being selected was
proportional to length of stay, sample quotas from each
project tend to be biased in favour of those finding the

project acceptable.   This bias is reflected in the fact
that those subjects who stayed at both WERC and Centrepoint were more positive about the project of interview.
The four Centrepoint males who had also previously stayed
at WERC preferred Centrepoint to the more formal regime of
WERC.   All but two of the six WERC males who had previously stayed at Centrepoint favoured WERC mainly because
of the longer length of stay:

> 'It [Centrepoint] seems pretty good, but I can't see
> what they're trying to do ... it's such short-term you
> couldn't stay there and get yourself a job.'

Twenty-five (73 per cent) from the WERC sample mentioned the material facilities as opposed to nine (31 per
cent) of the Centrepoint male sample and eight (27 per
cent) of the female sample.   On the whole, the clients
valued the facilities offered at WERC.   Eleven (32 per
cent) of WERC sample mentioned positively the cleanliness
of the Centre.   TV was also highly valued (26 per cent).
Eleven of WERC sample and eight at Centrepoint mentioned food or bed as an asset: 'it's a bed for the
night', 'it's a free bed and food'.   Three subjects from
WERC and four from Centrepoint criticised the food:

> 'I couldn't eat the breakfast, they gave you porridge
> with lumps the size of golfballs.' (WERC)

> 'The food's horrible, I can't eat it.   Could you eat
> it?' (Centrepoint)

Eleven per cent of WERC users noted the lack of sheets.
They varied widely in their reactions to the shower.
Some appreciated it for the chance of getting clean;
others disliked its compulsory nature, and the association
with screening for vermin:

> 'It's clean, but the strictness makes it clean.   Look-
> ing for lice put me off.   It was insulting.   It hurt
> my pride.'

> 'You have a shower - that's a good thing ... you get
> clean.   You might catch something walking around.'

Thirty per cent of the WERC sample complained about
staff attitudes.   There was criticism of the inquisitor-
ial nature of the questioning and the general lack of
respect:

'They don't treat you like men.'

'The staff degraded us.   Looked at us as absolute
tramps, as even worse than junkies.'

'It's an all right place, you just need to get rid of
the blokes that's in it.   They don't ask you to do
something, they tell you to do it.'

Many found interviews with Resettlement Officers a
necessary evil rather than an opportunity to make effective use of the resources.   Subjects adopted various
strategies to cope with the staff attitudes.   Mainly
these lay in passive resistance in the form of false information or minimal disclosure.   We know of at least
four who responded in this way, apart from those giving
false names and addresses:

'They're only social people.   You never want to take
them into your confidence because like the SS [social
security] they ask you questions and then think there's
another bloke who doesn't know what he's doing in
London.'

Centrepoint workers were viewed more positively as
being friendly, sympathetic and attentive.   Females
(34 per cent) valued this especially:

'Really nice people.'

'They are a shoulder to cry on.'

'They don't ask too many questions.'

Fewer males commented, but those who did (13 per cent)
were all positive.   One staff member in particular
attracted a great deal of praise from both sexes:

'I want to go back to London just to see her.   She was
great.   When she was there all the men used to be in
the office.' (female)

One male said:

'It was quite a laugh, the young girls [social workers]
there.   They were talking to me.   She was asking me
about football teams, you know, things I was interested
in.   I felt a fool, but it was nice really.'

Another dimension was the general atmosphere.   Centrepoint tended to be seen as informal and 'friendly'; WERC
as institutional, being likened to a 'prison', 'army bar-
racks' and 'concentration camp' by those most critical.

'It's [WERC] like a prison.   It's do this, do that the
whole time.   They seem to rub it in the whole time -
it's like signing on at the SS.'

'Centrepoint is a great place, a home from home, they
make you feel welcome.'

However, most WERC subjects did not refer to its institutional nature; perhaps because they took it for granted.   A few complained about not being allowed out once
admitted until the following morning.   Some complained
about having to do chores.
A few subjects criticised aspects of Centrepoint's
regime:

'The first time I stayed there, I was really scared
because they asked questions - where do you live,
what's your name, all behind the closed door ... I got
used to it ... the first time I was wondering what they
wanted in case they got the cops.   I didn't like the
boys and girls together.   I thought you could get
raped.' (female)

'I don't think they should have a mixed hostel.
That's where all the trouble starts.   When a lad and a
girl meets and they're lonely then anything can happen
... once they're outside the pearly gates of Centrepoint then the lad goes missing and she's left pregnant
with nine months ahead of her.   I've never seen anything like it, it's not right you know.' (male)

Fellow users played a part in shaping the atmosphere.
At Centrepoint, 24 per cent of the females and 13 per cent
of the males noted and valued the other users.

'It's a great atmosphere down there - sharing your last
fag and everything.' (male)

Some liked to make friends, have people to talk to or a
chance to make contacts.   Others specifically mentioned
the opportunities to meet the opposite sex.   Two males
mentioned the number of girls; one proudly stated how he
had 'had his all' at Centrepoint.   One female said: 'One
thing I'm certain of, I'll never be short of fellas here.'

Few Centrepoint subjects criticised the other users.   One
male however was scathing about the male users:

> 'They're all ponces, they go up to people and ask them
> for money.   I could never do that.'

WERC subjects were less happy with fellow users.
Seventeen per cent complained, describing some other users
as 'drunkards', 'con men' and 'dossers'.

> 'I had to sit back to back with these weirdos.   I was
> trying to eat my sausage and beans, and there were
> blokes slapping their bread and butter all over the
> place....   It made me sick.'

> 'It's no good - it's full of old codgers.'

Two WERC subjects however were complimentary.
'They're good fellas, you can have a laugh with the lads.'
The other who had recently stayed at Camberwell Reception
Centre was relieved to find 'decent people, not too many
drunks' as well as ones of his own age.
   Subjects assessed WERC and Centrepoint predominantly in
terms of their immediate need for food, shelter, entertainment and personal contact.   Relatively little emphasis was placed on longer-term help.   Five WERC subjects
(15 per cent) were critical about the lack of such help.
One man complained:

> 'It's a bed, they couldn't do much worse for you.
> They don't exceed the limit by helping you.   They're
> taking their time helping me.   They've only pushed two
> jobs my way.'

On the other hand, a few subjects saw WERC's indefinite
length of stay as in itself helpful.

> 'You can stay until you're back on your feet.'

> 'They give you a chance to get a job.'

   At Centrepoint, seven females (24 per cent) but only
one male mentioned the help they had been given;   only two
females commented on the lack of help.   These comments
were mainly concerned with jobs and accommodation and
being able to discuss problems.
   On the whole subjects staying at North were less critical.   Only two subjects complained.   A female said it
was 'dirty'.   A male said it was both dirty and cold.
He was also scathing about the other users:

'It's a dump, all the people there have been in prison
or something ... most of them take drugs ... I don't
like being stuck with people like that ... it gets
together all the people who are vagabonds and they
don't do anything for each other ... they just sink
further....   [People] should have discipline.'

The other subjects usually enjoyed the communal living
and put up with the material defects:

'I don't want no fancy bed or fancy blankets, I'm quite
satisfied with this now.   If I was settling down my
life would change like, but at the moment you can't
beat a bed like that ... I feel more at home with just
a mattress thrown on the ground.'

The staff were not commented on.   They seemed invisible.   One subject fought with a worker and was thrown
out but was allowed back the following night.   One female
mentioned the help received in squatting.

'For a while it was really organised and there was a
great bloke running it and then it all fell apart ...
Jimmy used it to open squats.   He'd see a place empty
and he'd just go and get in.'

Subjects' evaluations of the projects of interview compare favourably with those made of other agencies they had
stayed at.   The eight males who had experienced Salvation
Army hostels, were all strongly critical and mentioned no
redeeming features.   The main complaints concerned the
dirty nature of both hostels and users, the risk of infestation, inadequate facilities and the fact that users
tended to be noisy, drunk and aggressive.

'It's terrible ... full of dossers, I'd rather sleep
rough.'

'It was dirty ... the breakfast was cold and greasy, I
couldn't eat it ... I couldn't sleep for the noise.'

Two males had stayed at Camberwell Reception Centre.   One
found it a 'dirty place with lots of people taking drugs
and drinking'.   The other said it was 'a good place';   it
had fixed him up with a 'good job' and paid his fares.   A
female who had stayed at Camden Reception Centre found it
'too strict'.   Another had avoided it because she had
heard 'they bathe you in disinfectant and shove things up
you'.

Subjects tended to avoid lodging houses and other agencies where older users predominated. There were relatively few agencies offering emergency accommodation primarily to young homeless people. The only ones more than one of our sample had stayed at were Bit's crash pad, GALS and St Giles. The last two offered short-term accommodation for girls.

Bit's crash pad was appreciated for being non-selective and undemanding but the four males and one female who had stayed there all complained of a low standard of hygiene or comfort:

'I was grateful at the time as I was sleeping rough, but it doesn't compare with Centrepoint ... you just get blankets and bed down ... the window was frozen.'

'It was really crummy ... at least I didn't catch anything.'

The three females who stayed at GALS and the two at St Giles were all critical mainly because of the discipline and judgmental nature of the staff: for instance, 'too snobby', 'too strict'.

Subjects used a wide range of agencies offering advice or day centre facilities. The main ones used (before the initial interview) were: Soho Project (thirteen males and eight females), Bit (seven subjects), St Martin's (five subjects) and New Horizon (four subjects).

Soho Project and Bit were seen as the most helpful, Soho Project for finding jobs and Bit for general information. Centrepoint tended to refer many of its clients to the former - mainly for jobs. Two males had found jobs through this agency. Several subjects valued it as a place to meet friends and contacts in a relaxed atmosphere. Some however were indifferent to it:

'You get the same people going in there every day, the same ones you get in Centrepoint.... It's a load of rubbish.' (female)

New Horizon was liked for being 'friendly', 'they're really nice there', 'it's a good laugh', though one girl found other users frightening: 'they scared me. They all take drugs and things.'

We got little response from clients to questions about the way provision could be improved. Those questions sometimes confused and surprised:

'That's a very difficult question. I suppose I do use

these places but I always looked at them as for someone else.' (male)

'It's not their fault [Centrepoint] - they're doing the best they can.' (female)

Five subjects (three males and two females) felt there should be more Centrepoints.   Five more mentioned the lack of accommodation for couples.   Another two felt there should be more hostels for girls; two mentioned that there should be more hostels generally.   One female felt that Centrepoint finances would be better spent find-ing people a place to live rather than giving them a bed.
A few were more imaginative:

'The Government should set up centres like this [WERC] not just in London but in the main areas, but run in such a way that you don't get millions coming and say-ing they're destitute ... they should be places of rest from problems.' (male)

'You could have a huge day centre with a part for sleeping.   It could have a job bureau and an area for recreation, a canteen with half price meals.   It could act as a meeting place where people could go and iden-tify with each other because they're in the same situa-tion.'

To summarise: subjects did not seem very demanding of the projects of interview.   Expectations were usually narrowed to what the projects offered in the way of satis-fying immediate needs.   WERC was primarily valued for its material facilities, cleanliness and indefinite length of stay; Centrepoint for its friendly, informal atmosphere. The relief at finding somewhere to stay tended to dampen criticism, especially among those who had slept rough. Those few who had previously stayed in other agencies were often pleasantly surprised by the projects or at least relieved at finding them less unpleasant.   Criticism may also have been muted for other reasons.   Subjects may have wished to appear adaptable and resilient and to avoid giving the impression that they were carping, self-pitying or ungrateful.   'Beggars can't be choosers' and 'It's OK' were typical sentiments, especially among WERC subjects.
The main disadvantage of using WERC seemed to be disci-pline, formality, intrusion and patronising attitudes on the part of the staff.   Another but less significant drawback was the presence of older and/or disturbing users.   A large proportion complained about these

features.   However, the majority did not do so, partly
because they took them for granted.
     The main disadvantage of staying at Centrepoint was the
severely limited length of stay.   Instead of complaining
about this, subjects saw themselves as lucky to be staying
there.   The limit on the time they might stay - a point
continually emphasised by the staff - often created a
feeling of pressure and sometimes one of apprehension as
the deadline loomed nearer.   Disappointment was expressed
at not being allowed to stay longer.   However, subjects
tended to suspend their anxieties and instead to enjoy the
benefits of Centrepoint while they could.   Some subjects
invested more energy in trying to prolong their stay at
Centrepoint than in trying to find alternative accommodation.   They applied both persistance and pretence to this
end.   Any disenchantment with Centrepoint arising out of
the limited length of stay was not likely to be felt until
after re-admission had been refused.

Aims and practice

Centrepoint saw its main function as befriending and counselling.   Its 1974 'Annual Report' states: 'What the
young people who come to Centrepoint need most is the
chance to talk and be listened to in a friendly atmosphere.'   The project was intended both as a haven (protection, recovery, support) and a stepping stone to more
settled situations (re-orientation, advice and referral).
On the other hand, WERC saw its primary function as 'resettlement';   the key ingredient of this was employment.
Clients should be encouraged and helped to find work.
Their efforts to do so should be monitored so that where
relevant, pressure may be applied and 'abuse' of the project guarded against.
     However, there were conflicts between the avowed aims
of these agencies and the ways they worked in practice.
Most of WERC's effort went into the feeding and accommodating its clients rather than resettling them.   There
was often a delay of several days before clients saw the
Resettlement Officer, by which time many clients had left.
It sometimes took several weeks before clients were judged
to be 'not seriously trying to find work' and refused re-
admission.   Most subjects, however, did not see 'help'
from Resettlement Officers as particularly relevant and
the minority who did, found it inadequate.   For instance:

     'They've helped me as much as I wanted ... free food,
     good bed and TV.'

'The only help they give you is to get you up in the
morning and get you to work in the morning if you have
a job.   They don't even tell you you've been there too
long.'

Clients and agencies tended to have different, often
conflicting priorities.   For instance, our subjects were
often more concerned about satisfying their immediate
needs than availing themselves of any longer-term help
offered by the project.   The day-to-day business of survival and the need for recreation might take precedence
over efforts to assure the less immediate future.   The
West End, seen by Centrepoint as a potential 'trap',
tended to be valued by its clients.   What was intended as
'counselling' might be seen as casual chatting or prying.
Centrepoint was keen to limit the length of stay,
whereas clients were usually equally keen to prolong it.
This conflict of interests not only diverted attention
away from befriending and counselling but also undermined
the basis for these.   Clients misled workers (to ensure
admission and prolong length of stay).   Workers routinely
distrusted clients' stories and devoted much of their
energy to establishing if and for how long individuals
should stay.
In public, Centrepoint tended to proclaim its clients'
helplessness whilst being unable to relate this to daily
experience.   For instance, one Centrepoint worker explained the vulnerability of the client, giving a picture
of adolescent disturbance and describing their 'inner
journey' and need for 'emotional space'.   However, she
eventually said:

'You get disillusioned in the end you know.   You end
up sending them to WERC for a taste of reality.'

As a short-term project with long-term goals, Centrepoint was operating under considerable pressures and constraints.   Scarce resources obliged workers to ration
length of stay to a few days at the most.   They gave
preference to those who seemed most vulnerable or motivated to use Centrepoint as a springboard to more settled
situations.   They were anxious not to be taken advantage
of and to guard against being counterproductive.   For
instance, they did not want to lull clients into a false
sense of security or encourage young people to come to or
stay in the West End by providing a free 'hotel' and
social club.   These concerns are illustrated by the following entries made on the record cards of subjects:

'Very elusive character, seems indifferent about
things.   Does not give anything in conversation.
Centrepoint can't help.   Refer to WERC.'

'Not too worried about trying.   WERC in future.'

'Quite reasonable person....   Should be OK on his own.
Refer to WERC.'

'Suspect they're both cons ... suggest WERC.'

'Obviously down for a weekend in town.   Recommend not
to re-admit.'

'Accepting that "X" is on a low income and finds it
difficult to manage financially, if his life style includes soft drugs then he ought to get his priorities
right....   He's living beyond his means.   No re-
admittance.'

'Gave false name.   No re-admittance.'

There were severe limits on Centrepoint's capacity to
help its clients into more settled accommodation.   There
was a lack of suitable hostel accommodation.   Rented
accommodation was scarce and expensive.   Clients were
sometimes sent to specialised residential facilities, even
when they did not really qualify.   In most cases Centrepoint had little choice but to refer clients to other
forms of emergency accommodation and thus merely pass them
around the homeless circuit.   Table 7.4, based on records
kept on all the subjects who stayed at Centrepoint (not
only the ones interviewed there), illustrates Centrepoint's referral strategy.

TABLE 7.4   Referrals from Centrepoint

	Males	Females
Referred to WERC	5	1
Referred to Centrepoint hostel	5	-
Referred to other voluntary hostels	-	5
Referred to emergency shelter	-	1
Referred to hospital	-	1
Referred to advice agency	1	-
Referred to squat	1	-
Refused, no referral	8	4
Found own accommodation	3	3
Left London	6	3

	Males	Females
No information	7	12
Total	36	30

Both Centrepoint and WERC seemed to disperse clients unproductively.   They often made no referral at all (at least none that clients took advantage of) or were compelled to suggest other emergency accommodation.   This included accommodation of which they basically disapproved - for instance, lodging houses and in the case of Centrepoint WERC.   Referral was often used as a disciplinary strategy.

'A developing problem for many projects like Centrepoint is that of making positive referrals.' ('Annual Report', 1975)

ON THE HOMELESS CIRCUIT

Figure 7.1 shows the length of time the follow-up sample spent on the 'homeless circuit' whilst in London.   Included is any time spent in the types of emergency accommodation specified in Table 7.5, in the period between arriving in London and leaving.   In the case of the few who remained in London for more than a year, we have only included homeless spells occurring within a twelve-month period.   Excluded is time spent homeless on subsequent returns to London and time spent in squats.

Males (total 29)

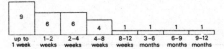

Females (total 16)

FIGURE 7.1 Length of time on the 'homeless circuit' (follow-up sample only)

Table 7.5 breaks down the time spent by the follow-up sample in the 'homeless circuit' into the various types of emergency accommodation used.   Unlike Figure 7.1, it excludes periods spent in the projects of interview.   The

TABLE 7.5 Types of emergency accommodation used (excluding squats): follow-up sample

	Males				Females			
	No. of people	No. of nights	Median no. of nights	Average	No. of people	No. of nights	Median no. of nights	Average
Reception centres	6	54	4	9	1	3	–	–
Emergency night shelters	9	16	1	1.8	1	13	–	–
Hostels/Lodging houses	5	252	24	50.4	6	218	14	36.3
Bed and breakfast	7	20	1	2.8	4	10	1.5	2.5
Crash pad	3	11	2	3.6	4	13	3	3.25
Friends' floors/ Casual contacts	5	31	3	6.2	7	88	14	12.5
Sleeping rough	13	116	4	8.9	7	51	5	7.3

average number of nights follow-up subjects spent in these
are: 10.3 (WERC subjects), 3.1 and 4.1 (Centrepoint males
and females) and 21 (North subjects).   Except in the case
of North these figures were checked against project
records.   The figures in both tables are unreliable because subjects often had difficulty remembering details.

We refer to a 'homeless circuit' because subjects
usually moved from one agency to another, often with
intervening spells sleeping rough or staying with befrienders and other contacts (sometimes on a sexual
basis).   Take for example the experiences of this girl,
who was aged seventeen, four months pregnant and accompanied by her boyfriend.   She stayed two nights at
Centrepoint and was refused a third night, spent instead
in the Marmite Shelter.   This was 'full of drunks' who
were 'filthy' and urinated on the floor.   When we initially interviewed her she was spending her fourth and
according to the staff positively her last night at
Centrepoint.   Up to this point she had also stayed one
night in the Sisters of Charity Hostel, one walking the
streets and two in a cheap 'hotel'.   She had had to leave
this because of a delay in receiving a social security
payment.   A girl at Centrepoint told her of a derelict
house in Victoria where she stayed two weeks until a man
there 'started causing trouble'.   She secured two further
nights at Centrepoint, one by persistently ringing the
door bell until finally admitted at 4 am and another by
giving a false name.   She was referred to a hostel by the
social services, where she stayed two days before deciding
to return home.

This girl's period in the homeless circuit was more unsettled than most.   More settled periods were more likely
to occur when subjects stayed at WERC, North and especially at lodging houses and longer-term hostels (for
instance, Charing Cross Hostel and Centrepoint's hostel
for younger males).

In Figure 7.1 we have excluded time spent in squats, because these tended to provide accommodation that was
relatively settled and independent.   The squats used were
mostly organised, with basic amenities.   In these respects squatting provided a means to leave the 'homeless
circuit' and so avoid dependency on the agencies, the
rigours of sleeping rough and associated insecurity and
constraints.   Apart from leaving London, it was the main
means used by the follow-up sample.   Eight males and five
females squatted during the period in question, the median
periods for males and females being thirty and twenty-
eight days respectively.   Two males and one female
squatted for more than six months.

SURVIVAL STRATEGIES

The main survival strategies discussed so far have involved sleeping rough or using agencies offering emergency
accommodation.   Below we look at some other major
strategies.

Squatting

This was a significant and fairly successful survival
strategy, used by thirteen follow-up subjects while remaining in London and by a further male on a subsequent
return to London.
    Squatting contacts were made through Bit, Release, and
the squatting grapevine.   The Elgin Avenue squatters were
very active in this period and had built a wide network of
squatting links.   Bit in West London had close links with
these networks and, in particular, with North (originally
a squat).
    One male subject trying to find accommodation for his
family became involved in the Elgin Avenue squats.   He
spoke of interviews with housing authorities:

    'They just dragged up your whole background, what you
    had for breakfast twelve months ago ... that sort of
    thing ... it was really bad....   Having answered all
    the questions then we were told there was a waiting
    list ... other squatters have been the most help to
    us.'

Employment

On the whole the individuals in Table 7.6 found unskilled
work.   The majority did not find work at all and those
who did were mainly in casual employment.
    Three members of the sample (two males and one female)
felt they had difficulties because of their physical
appearance:

    'I don't think I'll last a minute in that job.   I know
    that the minute I walk in there they'll see this dirty
    person walking in and they'll have second thoughts
    about it.'

    'I know why we haven't got a job, it's the way we
    dress - you can't get a job walking in like this.'

TABLE 7.6 Employment in London: numbers of those finding jobs according to length of time in London (follow-up sample only)

Length of time in London	Males				Females			
	Regular	Casual	None	Total	Regular	Casual	None	Total
Up to 1 week	-	-	3	3	-	-	2	2
Up to 2 weeks	-	1	1	2	-	-	1	1
Up to 1 month	-	1	2	3	-	1	1	2
Up to 6 weeks	-	2	2	4	-	-	1	1
Up to 2 months	-	-	1	1	-	-	2	2
Over 2 months	2	6	8	16	2	3	5	8
Total	2	10	17	29	2	4	12	16

One male complained that he could not get jobs as a
waiter because of the tattoos on his hands.   Living-in
work (chambermaids, kitchen-porters) was seen as a means
of solving both accommodation and employment problems.
One male who frequently returned to London after the
initial interview found this easy to get:

'It's dead easy to get them, you just wear a shirt and
tie and talk posh then you get a job just like that.
The pay isn't very good but you get accommodation and
meals which is what you want, you save your money so
you don't spend it.'

However, he was the exception, most found it difficult:

'It's more difficult than I expected to get a living-in
job.   There's others around like guards or shop assistants - that kind of thing - but no hotel jobs.'

The most immediate problem for those seeking work is
where to go.   Two men from Northern Ireland came from a
small village and expected to get employment immediately
by walking onto a building site:

'It wasn't like at home.   We didn't know where to
start looking.   We were walking round Trafalgar Square
and Piccadilly looking for factories or sites but we
couldn't find anything.'

(They went to living-in work in the North of England,
found through Centrepoint.)
Experience in finding work varied enormously.   One
girl, with a good educational background, unemployed for
several months in Ireland found London surprisingly easy:

'Your lot are angels.   When I wanted a job in London I
went to the Labour and she said pick a card - no - pick
three, you've got an interview with every one of them -
I got a job as a trainee accountant ... it was great.'

Her experience was exceptional.   For the majority (of
both sexes) if they did find employment it was poorly
paid.

'Work was very difficult to get, jobs were sheer and
utter boredom.' (male)

'I was scrubbing pots.   I didn't like it.   It was
pots, pots, pots and more pots, huge great things and I

see fellas younger than myself giving me the orders and
they make me scrub them again and again ... I didn't
like it ... I lasted three days.' (male)

'There could be more information about jobs - the only
job you could get was a cleaning job.' (female)

Keeping the job was the next problem.   There was normally a week's delay before receiving wages in regular
work.   The three-day rule on supplementary benefit claims
and discretionary payments made it difficult to obtain
money.   Some subjects found they could not afford fares
to and from work.

'I found a job down in South London but it cost me £1 a
day to get there, the social security wouldn't give me
nothing so how was I to get there.'

Those sleeping rough could not keep clean and were too
tired to work efficiently:

'I did have a job but I was sleeping out and it was so
cold I wasn't really sleeping much.   I used to go to
sleep in the day.   They didn't sack me but I left in
the end, I think they felt sorry for me.'

Many established a pattern - two or three days of
casual work followed by a couple of social security
claims, perhaps some petty crime to supplement their
income.   Many found it impossible to live on their wages
in London without supplementing it in some way:

'We didn't realise the wages would be so rubbish.   You
have to work for pennies down there.'

'I never had any money to do anything after food and
fares and rent, I had to stay in all the time.   That's
no way to live.'

Frequently, employers paid extremely low wages and were
involved in various tax and national insurance fiddles:

'I knew we'd be all right because we're girls ... the
bloke has given us a job and he's taken all the responsibility for taking us on without cards or anything.'

Social security

'The fact that a man does not have an address when he
calls at the local office is not in itself a reason for
refusing a payment....' ('Supplementary Benefits Hand-
book', 1972)

TABLE 7.7 Claims for supplementary benefit while still
'new' to London (follow-up sample only)

Length of time in London	Males			Females		
	Emer-gency claim	Full claim	Both	Emer-gency claim	Full claim	Both
Up to 1 week	-	-	-	1	-	-
Up to 2 weeks	1	1	-	-	-	-
Up to 1 month	1	1	-	1	-	-
Up to 6 weeks	-	-	1	-	-	-
Over 6 weeks	2	7	1	3	1	1
Total	4	9	2	5	1	1

Table 7.7 shows the number of follow-up subjects claiming benefit in the period up to two months after arrival.

The local office in Westminster was not dealing with
'no fixed abode' claims at the time of our sampling.
Claimants were normally referred to the lodging-house
offices (known as 'No Fixed Abode Offices') Thames North
and South.

'I walked all the way down there (Thames South office)
but then I couldn't face it when I saw all those men
coughing and spitting and pissing on the floor. I was
too scared to go in.'

'I wouldn't go there, not with all those dossers.'

Of twelve claims for discretionary emergency payments,
eight were unsuccessful:

'They've been rotten. I went down today and explained
to them ... I didn't have an appointment ... I told
them I had to pay board for this place [North] and that
I needed money for the fares to get to work and some
food and he just said "That's not an emergency.
Cheerio."'

'We went to four offices all over and none of them
would give us anything because we were "no fixed
address".'

One man receiving an emergency payment from the Thames
South office complained:

'They gave me £6.70 to try and find a bed-sitter which
is no good.'

Some claimed they had to wait for days before receiving
a giro, running a risk of losing any accommodation.
Others simply seemed to spend days waiting for an interview or being passed from one office to the next.
One male Centrepoint user registered at the Westminster
Employment Exchange. He was sent to Hammersmith where he
was told there were more jobs. He signed on and was referred to Hammersmith social security office with his Bl
to make a claim. He was referred back to Westminster
social security office as he had spent the last night in
their area and from there on to Thames South as an NFA
claimant. At Thames South he was issued with a voucher
for the Salvation Army with no cash. Walking from one
office to the next, this journey took three days.

'You go from one place to another place and by the time
your money comes through, it's [accommodation] just
gone.'

'They really should tighten up the social security
system in London. I went down to Settles Street, then
to Scarborough Street. I had one penny in my pocket
and I hadn't eaten all day. It took all day and all
they gave me was 57p and a voucher for the Sally Army.'

Counter clerks seemed very cautious about giving emergency payments. One told us that 50 per cent of such
claims were phoney. Another that 'It wouldn't hurt them
to do without for a couple of days. It might teach them
not to do it again.' Several expressed the view to us
that such payments might encourage young people into a
homeless way of life. One pregnant homeless girl walked
three miles to an office to be informed that 'there are
people much worse off than you'.
Discussions with workers in the homeless agencies informed us that claims for clients were greatly helped if
there was a good working relationship with the counter
clerks. A note or phone call could ease the process.
The high turnover of SBC counter staff as well as agency
workers hindered the development of this relationship.

A minority of subjects praised the help received from
various offices:

'They've always been helpful [North London office].
I've nothing to complain about.'

'I've always found them very good here.   They gave us
£5.   That's more than you'd get up in Glasgow.'

They became skilled at packaging their identity and exploiting the system.   One male was proud of his skill at
conning SS offices.   He claimed to have received over £60
at Thames South office by giving false names and addresses.

'I've got this way of getting money out of people;   the
right words come out.   I was telling him a load of
bullshit.'

Two males and one female were fiddling social security
claims.   One man staying at WERC was illegally receiving
money from Thames South office.   WERC does daily 10 per
cent checks to guard against this.
A small number declined to claim benefits which were
their right:

'I don't believe in it [claiming benefit].   My
father's never done it in his life and I'm never going
to.   I'd rather go stealing.'

In addition to the follow-up information, we know from
the first interview that twelve males and four females had
already made social security claims.   Six of these were
for emergency payments of which four were successful.
Two of those receiving no payment were referred to WERC.

Crime and prostitution

Our information is based both on initial and follow-up
interviews.   It is bound to understate the extent of deviance because we simply do not have information on most
subjects after the first interview.
Three males and one female were stealing from punters -
men enticed into alleyways for sex and then set on by male
accomplices.   Another female went 'mugging' twice with a
friend at Victoria Station.

'We was really depressed, really scruffy.   You should

have seen us the first time we came down ... I felt
like killing anybody.   It was after my first lot of
clothes were ripped off [stolen]....   We were skint.
We went down there [Victoria].   She was a lesbian.
We nearly battered her to death with her umbrella.
We got about £3 off her.   We done it again but they
put a warrant out for us.'

Most offences seemed part of a survival strategy:

'I was kind of hungry.   I had no money or nothing.   I
hadn't had a proper meal for so long, just bits of
cheese, and I went down to the supermarket, just took a
few things - that was all right and started making
regular calls to that shop ... I got caught ... I could
have got away but thought where am I going to sleep
tonight.'

We know that eight males and two females received sentences while homeless in London.   Of the males one was
fined for possession of drugs (physeptone);   three were
placed on probation (two charged with theft and one for
loitering with intent) and four received custodial sentences - two for burglary, one for theft with an offensive
weapon, and another for breaking and entering.   For these
males, the median length of their homeless period in
London was seven weeks.   The two females were convicted
for assault on a police officer and soliciting respectively.   Both were remanded for short periods in Holloway
Prison.
    We know that five females and three males engaged in
prostitution while homeless in London.   We strongly suspect that a further two females were soliciting.   Three
further males claimed to live by 'rolling punters' (leading on homosexuals and then mugging them or taking the
money and running).   We suspect this figure is an under-
estimate, subjects would be reluctant to admit it.   It is
a reasonably common survival strategy used on the homeless
scene.   'They all do it', one subject told us.   'Most
people do it for a while', another female said.
    None were involved in organised prostitution.   'Punt-
ers' were generally picked up on the streets and amusement
arcades in the Piccadilly area.   One or two went further
afield to King's Cross.   The pick-up places shifted
according to police activity and were monitored by the
grapevine.   Newcomers often introduced to the scene by
older members were initially reluctant, but persuaded by
economic considerations.   One female found the money hard
to resist:

'When she told me she got £15 for five minutes we went
down to the Mecca and I had to go with five of them ...
I got ripped off ... it was first time.   When I came
back I took a whole load of barbs and went down the
Apple [all-night café/club] and cried.   It didn't put
me off it ... I don't know why I do it really.   I just
do it for the money, I love my clothes.'

This sixteen-year-old girl was on the scene for over a
year and was arrested several times for soliciting.   She
spent the money on clothes and horse riding which she
loved.   She eventually returned home for a while and
found work in a factory.   She still returned to London
picking up punters at weekends, telling her parents she
was staying with friends.   She also successfully encouraged two other girls from her home town to join.   She was
the only female for whom it became a career.   Others used
it periodically for quick money.   No female found the experience pleasurable.   It was to be endured rather than
enjoyed:

'Even now I don't enjoy sex, it's like other things to
me, like brushing your teeth.'

'I couldn't bear him near me, I was clenching my fist.
Every one I go with, I scream.'

One girl had an abortion at five months, which was
badly done and resulted in protracted spells in hospital.
The male subjects were even more reluctant to discuss
their experiences.   One in the follow-up interview expressed disgust for homosexuals and the 'Dilly' boys in
particular.

'You'd be better off getting them in the street and
killing them ... I didn't like the homosexual thing
... I've got too much pride ... well I suppose some of
them are all right really.   Well I did it for a bit.
You've got to do something, but I didn't like it,
that's why I got a job in the end.'

One male was more open:

'I had no scruples about doing anything to survive.
I have been on the game to try it out.   If there
was no WERC I would do it to get food.'

He would do it again 'if absolutely necessary.   If I was
emotionally rock bottom ... if I could find the hardness.'

Friends/contacts

Soho Project and Centrepoint were valued especially as a
source of friends and fresh contacts.   The grapevine was
vital for information about sleeping places, squats and
possible jobs.   The General Household Survey (1973)
showed that of people under twenty-five in their present
jobs for less than twelve months in the GLC area, 32 per
cent found work through relations/friends as compared with
only 5 per cent through employment exchanges and 12 per
cent through private agencies.   One difficulty for these
homeless young people was that they had so few contacts in
the London area.
    Twenty-three males (32 per cent) and six females (17
per cent) mentioned feeling lonely in the initial
interview.

    'You don't make any friends at Dean St [WERC], just
    acquaintances.   I've been really lonely in London.   I
    want some company.   I just go around all day on my
    own.   How do you meet people here?   It seems such a
    large place, everyone is in their own scenes.' (male)

    'I feel disappointed by it [London].   You get terribly
    depressed, but you think that something will happen
    today.   The loneliness is getting through to me.'
    (female)

    'You never see the same person twice, everyone is mov-
    ing on.   If you see a girl and you take a fancy to
    her, you'll never see her again.' (male)

    In several cases loneliness severely undermined their
morale.   It partly prompted two females to attempt suicide - one on her subsequent return to London and the
other, who slashed her wrists in a Piccadilly Circus lava-
tory, before she got to stay at Centrepoint.   On the
whole, the females were less lonely because they were much
more likely to come to London accompanied by a friend or
partner.   A few other subjects had more complex views
about isolation:

    'Sometimes I feel I just don't want friends.   I just
    want to cry and do what I want to do on my own.'
    (female)

    'London is the worst city for solitude.   It's depres-
    sing but not for me.   I don't feel lonely, a bit de-
    pressed at times because I don't know anyone but being
    alone doesn't bother me.' (male)

Some subjects found it easier to make friends than at home:

'It's easy to make friends 'cos you're all in the same boat.' (female)

'It's probably a bit easier making friends in London, people are a bit lonelier, aren't they?' (male)

One girl who had got out of the West End scene still felt a strong pull to return eighteen months later. She felt her real friends were there and work bored her. She still returned to the West End on odd nights or at weekends knowing that she would meet old contacts.
She had been sixteen on arrival in London and was 'rescued' by a West End regular. He befriended her, gave her some money and later bullied her out of London in her own interests. Soho Project workers said it was not uncommon for older scene members to help newcomers in this way. This particular 'Samaritan junky' acted as an unpaid social worker.
Some encounters had a darker side. Subjects were beaten up by contacts and were pressured to solicit and become involved in petty crime. Most avoided provision where they might be associated with 'dossers', 'tramps' or 'winos'. However, one young girl sought out the company of 'tramps' and another male frequented the soup runs enjoying fetching soup for 'the old girls. I used to enjoy it. It would be my good deed for the day.'

Survival strategies: benefits and risks

These strategies helped to relieve or overcome the material and psychological problems of survival. The 'here-and-now' attitude adopted by most has a strong survival value. Squatting offers an immediate practical answer to lack of accommodation. Petty crime and prostitution can ameliorate destitution. By maximising personal resources, the homeless young person can maintain some degree of independence and anonymity and free himself of external demands that he may be unwilling or unable to fulfil:

'You stay there [WERC] too long and you get too institutionalised ... you wouldn't depend on yourself. You'd go back and depend on them all the time.... You'd go to the dogs; you don't get very much money; you're told what to do every five minutes, not given a chance to think for yourself - eventually something's

got to click somewhere and then you wouldn't care anymore.' (male)

The main costs of that survival are the risk of prose-
cution for a whole range of offences - petty theft, soliciting, drug offences, vagrancy, loitering with intent,
drunk and disorderly and offences related to squatting.
There are also health risks - malnutrition, pregnancy
whilst homeless, VD, lice.   Physical violence is not uncommon on the squatting scene or in the world of prostitution.   There is also a further risk of being labelled as
inadequate or delinquent and cut off from conventional
long-term solutions like obtaining reasonable accommodation and employment.   Homelessness and dependency on the
agencies may become a career that becomes increasingly
difficult to terminate:

'After six months day in day out routine of homeless,
your mind gets like a cat, incapable of thinking for
yourself any more - it's because they [for instance,
WERC] don't get to the bottom of it.   This is what I
mean by help.   Finding out why you are homeless and
jobless.' (male)

Two girls were pressurised (unsuccessfully) to go on
the game for men.   A West Indian pushed one (who was
jumping bail) against a wall:

'He threatened to strangle me.   He said "You're going
to be my woman".   He threatened me with a broken
bottle ... he dragged me by the hair up an alleyway and
threatened to have me ... he hit me in the face and
bruised my throat ... I had to live like that [hanging
around sleazy clubs].   I had no card for a job.   I
couldn't get a job and I couldn't get dole.'

'Some of the boys in Centrepoint, they ask you to take
punters down the street, then they jump on them and run
away with the money.'

THE TOTAL LENGTH OF TIME IN LONDON AND REASONS FOR LEAVING

Figure 7.2 shows the total length of time our follow-up
sample spent in London in the twelve-month period following arrival.   Five males and four females stayed in
London for the whole of this period.   A further twelve
males and six females in our follow-up sample left and
subsequently returned to London within this period.

Males

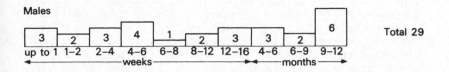

Total 29

Females

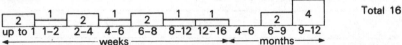

Total 16

FIGURE 7.2   Total length of time in London (follow-up sample only)

Table 7.8 gives the follow-up sample's main stated reasons for leaving London on the first or only occasion.

TABLE 7.8   Main stated reason for leaving London (follow-up sample only)

	Males	Females
Lack of accommodation	4	3
Lack of work	3	2
Picked up by the police	5	1
To avoid arrest	3	-
Lonely/lack of friends	1	1
Return to institution	1	2
Disillusioned with London	3	2
Other reasons	4	1
N/A (Still in London after twelve months)	5	4
Total	29	16

The 'other' category includes one male who returned with his pregnant wife to her home town. She wanted to have the baby at home. (She is the female in the 'other' category.) One male returned home to get married; another was encouraged to leave by his homosexual partner. The remaining male left London to chase a man who had stolen his money, whilst staying in a squat together.   He

went to Scotland to find him.   After failing, he visited
his parents and decided to stay and 'enjoy home comforts'.
   Three males picked up by the police were arrested for
offences committed while in London and were given prison
sentences in other areas (one deported to Eire).   The
other three subjects in this category had been on the run
and were returned to face trial in their home towns.

TABLE 7.9   Accommodation on the night prior to leaving
London (follow-up sample only)

	Males	Females
Centrepoint	4	1
WERC	4	-
Sleeping rough	3	2
Squat	5	2
Flat	3	-
With friends/relatives	1	2
Hostel	1	3
Prison	2	-
Not known	-	2
Living-in job	1	-
Those still in London after twelve months	5	4
Total	29	16

   Table 7.9 shows the accommodation status of those
leaving London on the night prior to their departure
(first time of leaving only).   Two males living in flats
left London through lack of employment;   the other lost
his flat when arrested on a visit to his parents.   The
male with a living-in job left to avoid arrest;   he had
been stealing from the hotel where he was working.
   All but two males and one female were unemployed at the
time of deciding to leave.   The two males were employed
only on a casual basis.   The female was in regular employment as a chartered accountant and left after being
badly frightened by threats on her life while staying in a
squat.
   Only two males and two females were established in independent rented accommodation in London twelve months
after arrival.   One female shared a bed-sit with a friend
and the other a small rented room with her husband and
baby.   One male shared a flat with friends and another
with his girl-friend.   All but the latter male had stayed
in London through the twelve-month period.   A further
five males had found flats or bed-sits in London but sub-

sequently left London.   All but one of those successfully
finding such accommodation in London did so through
friends or relatives.
   A further four males and two females had lived in
London for the whole twelve-month period.   Two males were
squatting.   One female was living with her parents, although she had spent most of the year in squats.   She had
returned to her parents (not seen for four years) when her
squat had been wrecked.   One male was serving a second
spell in prison (for possessing an offensive weapon).   He
had spent over two-thirds of the year inside prisons in
London and the rest of it homeless.   The remaining male
and female had lived largely off prostitution.   The
female was still homeless.   The male was living with an
ex-client, a man he had picked up in the West End.
Before this he had lived for eight months in St Mungo's
Charing Cross Hostel.

RETURNS TO LONDON

Twelve male and six female members of our follow-up sample
subsequently returned to London within the twelve-month
period.   Of these, seven males and two females made
London a base for at least three months.   Two of these
males and both the females were still in London at the end
of the twelve-month period.   One female secured a living-
in job as a nanny before setting out for London again.
The other female was homeless for a while before moving in
with a man who later threw her out.   She ended up in a
mother-and-baby-home.   Four of the males found independent rented accommodation after returning and another a
squat for his drug-dealing.   Another male, who spent the
summer months touring with a fairground, used London as a
base during the winter months.
   Five males and four females returned for usually much
shorter periods.   One male, for instance, came to 'escape
myself and my responsibilities'.   He had done this periodically over the course of the last six years.   He
called it a 'disappearing act'.   At the follow up, he
felt he was near to 'breaking the habit'.   After eighteen
months of unemployment, he had just found a job as a ware-
houseman.   His desire to break the habit was strength-
ened by an experience on his last visit:

   'I saw a guy on drugs, he looked like he was dying.   I
   thought that could happen to me ... I hitched straight
   back.'

Two females ran away to London after rows with boyfriends. They both took their babies and were homeless.
One only stayed four days and returned 'for the child's
sake' and because her boyfriend offered to marry her.
The other collapsed with a haemorrhage, was hospitalised
and returned home. One female returned shortly after
leaving the first time, attempted suicide and went home.
The fourth female returned several times - she had become
involved in the West End scene and stayed with prostitutes
and drug addicts met there and was taking 'speed and
sleepers'. She eventually returned home.
Of all those returning to London, all but one male and
one female were homeless again on arrival. Some people
were adamant about never returning to London unless certain pre-conditions were met:

> 'No, only for a day, I don't want to get into trouble,
> I've had enough, I've been clean for two years ... I
> don't want to get involved with roughs and get in
> trouble with the police ... I didn't care about the
> dangers then I could have been strangled. Now I'm
> scared I'm wised up. I won't go up to stay unless
> I've got a job first and worked to get a flat ... I
> like the bright lights, but I don't like the roughs
> that cause problems.' (female)

> 'I'd like to go back for a nostalgic wander round if I
> have the money this summer ... I'll stay at Centrepoint
> because it's free ... I'd like to go back and stay but
> I'd have to have qualifications.' (female)

RETROSPECTIVE VIEWS OF LONDON

Many of the follow-up sample had mixed feelings about
London. They may have enjoyed the speed and excitement
but found it difficult to survive. Some made a distinc-
tion between being homeless in London and being in work
and settled there. Four males and three females fell
into this category. One male felt London was:

> '... big, vicious, fast. There are more opportunities
> there ... I felt more accepted there. Nothing seems
> odd to Londoners, everything happens in London [music]
> ... we're thinking of trying to exchange our flat in a
> couple of years' time ... we'd do it properly next
> time.'

Another said he could only live there if accommodation was
found:

'I'd live there but I'd have to have a flat or a house ... I like the night life, the speed ... it's on the ball ... new clothes would hit London before anywhere else. You can get the trend straight away ... it takes twelve months to get here ... that's a long time ... I'd live there but there are too many memories ... too many things gone wrong ... you meet the same old guys and girls all doing the same thing either skiving or knocking off stupid things from shops.'

Seven males and four females had a largely negative evaluation of London. They had been disappointed and disillusioned and found the experience of homelessness there depressing and demoralising. One male subject could hardly bear to talk about it.

'I hate the place, I hate the people. They're dead ignorant, I've got no time for them. It's unfriendly. Everybody is after your money ... I saw some sights I'll never forget. It's a real rip off. I'd rather forget about it.

He had spent five months in London altogether - three months in the Centrepoint hostel and found a flat. He did not leave voluntarily but was forced to give up his flat when arrested for the theft of a giro on a visit to his home town.
Another disliked the whole experience:

'There are no bright lights or anything down there. It's just one big expensive town. I have no good memories of it. The town is too big. It's not the place to get stuck.'

and one felt his drug problem had been aggravated:

'London burns your fingers. I would think twice before doing it again. Life is such a hang-up there that I'd have a jack [fix] and forget about it.'

The feeling of loneliness was often mentioned:

'I used to ask the time of day and people used to walk right by you. If I'd made a load of friends I'd probably have said London was a great place, like students do. They can go to one house in one part of it and another in another part to see people they know.'

and the frustration caused by the inaccessibility of different life-styles:

'It felt bad ... you're walking around and looking at
all those posh fellas and looking at them get through
all that money and you've got nowhere to go ... it
gives you a sort of pain inside.'

For a small minority in the follow-up sample, their experience in London had been a welcome break from the mono-
tony or drudgery in their home towns.   It had been a
jaunt, and 'experience':

'It made me feel happy, made me feel a bit at ease ...
just walking about seeing new things, different places
to go.   Taking a different view of life instead of
being stuck in Leicester or Glasgow.'

'If I had the same life to lead I'd do it all over
again ... I had a good time.'

We asked most of the follow-up sample what or whom had
been most help to them while homeless in London.   In many
cases, subjects gave no clear answers.   In some cases
they felt they had received no help or did not see the
questions as relevant:

'I never really wanted any help, not really ... you
look to someone for help once and you're going to rely
on that person all the time for help.   You're just
going to say to hell with it.   I'll let somebody else
get on with it.   There comes a time when you have to
do it for yourself ... in London I needed plenty of
money and no more help than I can get for myself.'

Centrepoint was mentioned by five of the males and five
of the females as being most helpful.   One girl felt it
was most useful by introducing her to her befriender, an
older member of the West End scene who had been her 'salvation'.   She had used and abused Centrepoint during the
four months on the homeless circuit, using it as a meeting
place and social club:

'I used to love it ... when we were there it was the
same crowd every night, night after night.   We were so
close.   We was going out drinking together and eating
together.   We got in with them.   We used to make
people coffee.   We used to make them feel as though
they were wanted.   I really did enjoy it.   I missed
it.'

We found that some of the sample's assessments contras-

ted with those given at the time of the initial interview.
One man who had been very critical of WERC now saw things
differently:

'I think Dean Street was a sanctuary now in a way.
You were in there from 5 o'clock in the evening until
half past seven in the morning. You got a meal and a
bed ... the bed isn't much, but it keeps you out of
trouble.'

Another, who had been less than enthusiastic:

'For people that was coming in I think Dean Street was
doing a bloody good job. A lot of them was buggering
it up for themselves ... they were very fair to me ...
you had two TVs to watch and you got your meals.'

One girl who had enjoyed the friendliness and hospital-
ity of Centrepoint now criticised it:

'It was easy. It was too easy. You could do what
ever you liked ... plenty of fags and things.'

Several subjects were critical of the help offered:

'Centrepoint helped. The social services were no
good, social security were all right. We wouldn't
have survived if they hadn't given us the money. It
wasn't enough though. The social services sent us to
a hostel for homeless couples. It was terrible.
There were mattresses on the floor. It was like a
squat. I think if the social services had done more
for us it would have been better ... we would have been
determined to work then if we knew we were being given
a chance.'

'The social - they know how expensive it is in London.
They should give you enough money to live. If they do
give you money it's barely enough to cover the cost of
renting and then you've got no money for food. It
doesn't matter to them.'

'You need some place to stay that wasn't a "doss
house". You get treated like a dosser even though
you are not a dosser.'

'If they could do more for homeless people, not just
send them to these hostels. They don't care what
kind. Often it's just another squat with mattresses

and they call it a hostel.   It doesn't matter where
you're living as long as they get peace so you don't
keep pestering them.   They should give you a good flat
and give you a start.'

A few subjects assumed the perspective of the helper.

'If there's discipline, then you'll only get the people
who really need to be helped - who want to help themselves ... the people there [North] were there because
it's cheap and you get food even if the place is mangy.
They don't mind.   They can say they've got an
address.'

'That's a job [working at Centrepoint] I wouldn't mind
doing.   You could compare your own experiences with
theirs.   You might even be able to help them in some
respects.'

Chapter 8

FOLLOW UP

This chapter deals with experiences of the follow-up
sample in the twelve-month period following the initial
interview.   (Some of these have already been considered
in 'Time in London'.)   First we look at how we relocated
subjects and the nature of the sample obtained.

THE FOLLOW-UP SAMPLE

We re-interviewed twenty-nine (40 per cent) of the male
sample and sixteen (46 per cent) of the females.   These
re-interviews were scheduled for one year after the initial interview, but since our subjects were hard to
locate, they often occurred after a much longer period,
extending, in one case, up to two years.   Two males were
re-interviewed in prison: as the regulations forbade
tape-recorders, the interviewer went as a normal visitor
and took notes.   One emigrant to Australia was interviewed by post.
    We obtained information on the whereabouts of a further
ten males and four females, at some point at least one
year after the initial interview.   This was through con-
tacting probation officers, social workers, parents or
friends.   We refer to this group as 'traces'.   Since we
usually do not have comprehensive data on these, we exclude them from the tables and statements referring to the
follow-up sample - with the exception of the 'method of
relocation' table below - and mention them separately
where relevant.
    The largest proportions were relocated through an
address given to us at the initial interview, usually that
of a parent, and through probation officers or social
workers.

TABLE 8.1   Method of relocation (includes 'traces')

	Males	Females
Recontact address	17	10
Probation officer or social worker	15	3
DHSS records	2	3
Circulating agencies	2	4
Friends	1	-
Other	2	-
Total	39	20

We liaised with the records branch of the Department of Health who helped in forwarding letters from us.   The 'other' category includes one man found by chance - he had married someone from the female sample as we discovered on interviewing her.   He was living under a different name and still on the run from the police.   The second male in this category arrived voluntarily at our Greek Street office asking for his re-interview.

Representativeness of the follow-up sample

There could be systematic differences between our follow-up sample and our total sample.   We could be more likely to find those with a criminal record as relocation was made easier when our subjects told us they were on probation.   Fifteen of those re-interviewed or traced (fourteen males and one female) were relocated through the probation service.   One index of whether or not the follow-up and total samples were different lies in the proportions of those with criminal records at the time of the initial interview.

TABLE 8.2   Most serious sentence received before initial interview for both whole and follow-up sample

	Males		Females	
	% of whole sample	% of follow-up sample	% of whole sample	% of follow-up sample
Custodial	31.9	51.7	2.9	-
Supervision	11.1	10.4	14.2	18.8
Minor	20.8	20.7	5.7	12.5
None	36.2	17.2	77.2	68.8

In the whole sample, 64 per cent of the males and 23
per cent of the females had received some kind of convic-
tion prior to the initial interview, whereas the follow-up
sample showed a rate of 83 per cent and 31 per cent.   The
incidence of males with past custodial sentences is 20 per
cent higher in the follow-up than in the whole sample.
Those with past custodial sentences are more likely to receive further periods of imprisonment and thus be 'cap-
tive' subjects.   (Custodial sentences also indicate a
greater involvement with criminal processes and thus
whereabouts are more likely to be known to the probation
service - ten out of fifteen males with past custodial
sentences were relocated through the probation service.)
Those telling us in the initial interview about prison
sentences could have been more likely to be honest about
other details such as name and recontact address.

TABLE 8.3 Age proportions in the whole sample and follow-
up sample at initial interview

Age	Males		Females	
	% of whole sample	% of follow- sample	% of whole sample	% of follow- up sample
15	1.4	3.4	8.6	12.4
16-17	8.3	6.9	37.1	43.8
18-19	40.3	20.7	34.3	18.8
20-21	29.2	44.8	8.6	12.5
22-23	13.9	13.8	2.8	-
24-25	6.9	10.4	8.6	12.5

These are the ages given at the time of the initial
interview.   The age breakdowns for the whole and follow-
up samples are roughly similar with two exceptions.   The
male follow-up sample under-represents the 18-19 age group
and over-represents the 20-21 age group.   The female
follow-up sample under-represents the 18-19 age group.

TABLE 8.4 Breakdown of whole sample and follow-up sample
by project of initial interview

Project of interview	Males		Females	
	% of whole sample	% of follow- up sample	% of whole sample	% of follow- up sample
WERC	47.2	51.7	~	-
Centre- point	40.3	34.5	82.8	75.0
North	12.5	13.8	17.2	25.0

The breakdown of both samples by projects is basically similar.

Veracity

The follow-up subjects tended to have given correct names and re-contact addresses.   Only one of those re-interviewed gave a false name at the initial interview.   One male had given his correct name but false address, although the correct name and address of his probation officer.

Some subjects gave us a fuller or corrected picture in the follow up explaining why they had lied in the first interview.   For example, one girl who had invented two years of homelessness and lied about her age told us this was to cover running away from home.

One male packaging reasons for coming to London in terms of a religious missionary expedition told us he had really left through conflict with his wife.   A further three males told us they had been on the run.   One girl was ashamed and surprised when reminded of her stories. She had concocted an elaborate fantasy about her background:

> 'Oh I didn't say that, did I?   How awful, I'm blushing, none of that is true.'

One female initially refused to admit that she had already been interviewed.   We called at her house having been given her new address by her parents.   She had a new husband and did not want any previous history to be known to him.   She relented later and told us a fuller story including her real reasons for leaving home.

GEOGRAPHICAL LOCATION

Twelve months after the initial interview, thirteen males and eight females were living in what had been their last settled base (LSB) before they came to London.   Seven males and six females were in London twelve months later - one male being in prison there.   Six males were in penal institutions outside London - three in prisons close to their LSB.   Only three males (excluding the prisoners) and two females were not either in London or their LSB; of these one male and one female were settled abroad. The largest category is those who spent less than two months in London and returned to what had been their last

settled base prior to the initial interview, where they
remained for the year except for brief spells.   This includes nine males and seven females.   Their experience of
London had been as a jaunt or salutory experience.   Of
these, six males and four females had the intention of
staying for a longer term during the initial interview.
   The second largest group were those remaining in London
with only brief spells elsewhere.   This includes five
males and four females.   Third, there were those with no
settled base in the twelve months.   This includes six
males and one female.   The female spent most of the year
travelling abroad with her husband.   Two males expressing
a desire to settle down at the initial interview now rejected that.
   A further six males were immobile through being in institutions for eight or more months of the year.   Two
females and one male returned home for a minimum period of
three months and then came back to London, where they were
twelve months after the initial interview.   One male and
one female had settled abroad.   The female settled in
South Holland after being homeless in Amsterdam and the
man went home to Jersey for three months before emigrating
to Australia.   Another male and female married each other
while in London and returned, after nine months, to her
last settled base.

ACCOMMODATION

Figure 0.1 shows subjects' accommodation statuses twelve
months after the initial interview and compares them to
those at the time of their deciding to leave what had been
(prior to the initial interview) their last settled base.
   It is difficult to say whether our sample, taken as a
whole, improved or lowered their accommodation status between the two points in time.   The main changes were:
seven males in prisons, but five fewer subjects (three
males and two females) in other institutional settings
(ie probation hostel, psychiatric hospital and community
home);   three males in squats, two females in living-in
jobs, two females and one male in homeless family units
(under 'homeless'), but ten fewer subjects (six males and
four females) dependent for accommodation on parents,
relatives or friends.   The number in privately rented
accommodation rose from four to five for males and from
three to four for females.   However, privately rented
accommodation might not be so much of an improvement.
Some were paying high rents for poor housing.   One female
was living with her husband and small baby in a tiny damp
bed-sitter in North London, paying £7 a week.

Males

Accommodation at time of deciding to leave L.S.B.:	Accommodation status 12 months after first interview										
	Living with parents	Living with friend/relative(s)	Council flat	Own or rented accommodation	Lodgings	Homeless	Squat	Hostel (probation) and Aftercare	Psychiatric hosp. or comm. home	Prison	Totals
Living with parents	7			2			1	1		2	13
Living with friend/relative(s)		1		1						1	3
Council flat			1								1
Own or shared privately rented accommodation				1	1	1	1				4
Lodgings											—
Homeless	1									1	2
Squat											—
Hostel (Probation and Aftercare)										2	2
Psychiatric hospital or community home				1			1				2
Not applicable (no L.S.B. since leaving prison)	1									1	2
Totals	9	1	1	5	1	1	3	1	—	7	29

Females

Accommodation at time of deciding to leave L.S.B.:	Accommodation status 12 months after first interview							
	Living with parents	Living with friends/relative(s)	Own or shared rented accommodation	Homeless	Hostel (Mother and Baby)	Living-in job	Psychiatric hospital	Totals
Living with parents	1	1	3	2				7
Living with friends/relative(s)	1					1		2
Own or shared privately rented accommodation	2		1					3
Homeless				1				1
Hostel (Probation or Mother and Baby)				1	1			2
Living-in job								—
Psychiatric hospital						1		1
Totals	4	1	4	4	1	2	—	16

FIGURE 8.1 Accommodation status twelve months after first interview compared with that in LSB prior to first interview

As Figure 8.1 shows, only ten males and four females
had the same accommodation status in their LSB as at
twelve months after the first interview (in eight cases
living with parents).   To get a fuller picture of the
follow-up subjects' accommodation experience over the
twelve-month period, we broke down the information into
the longest period spent in any one form of accommodation
(called main accommodation type).

TABLE 8.5   Main accommodation type used in the twelve-
month period following initial interview

	Males	Females
Parental home	6	3
Penal institution	9	-
Private rented	4	4
Homeless agencies	3	1
Squat	2	1
Homeless family unit	1	2
Living-in job	-	2
Council flat	1	-
Lodgings	1	-
Probation hostel	1	1
Psychiatric hospital	1	-
Living with friends	-	1
Travelling abroad	-	1
Total	29	16

Table 8.5 shows that nine males (31 per cent) spent a
longer time in prison than in any other type of accommodation.   Of these, six spent eight or more months in prison
over the period, and four served more than one spell.

Only four males and four females used privately rented
accommodation as their main accommodation resource.   Two
males and two females had flats or bed-sits in London, the
remainder outside London.   Of the latter, one male was in
a flat in Australia, and the other male shared a flat with
friends in his home town.   Both females had found rented
rooms with great difficulty.   One was living with her
boyfriend in a small room in her home town, costing £9 a
week paid out of social security.

Six males and three females used their parental home as
their main accommodation resource.   Of these, three males
and two females had talked of conflict with parents before
leaving London.   One male who had wanted to get away from
his parents at the time of the first interview found he
kept coming back: 'Everytime I came for a visit, I ended
up stopping, I missed the place.'

He had found a flat and a job in London and gave it up to
return home to parents.   At the time of re-interview
overcrowding was causing conflict between himself and his
brothers and there were regular fights.
    Reconciliation with parents was sometimes made easier
by a period away.   After five months away, most of it
spent homeless in London, one male subject returned home:

> 'I couldn't take it any more.   I was sick, really sick
> and I asked them if they would take me in ... they
> could see what a state I was in so they let me stay.'

He stayed six months but at the follow-up interview was
not totally reconciled to living at home.   There was
still tension between him and his stepfather:

> 'It's not much better now ... you can feel the hostili-
> ty, I don't really like him and he doesn't really like
> me ... I don't know where else to go let's face it ...
> what I want to do now is get a flat.   I'm trying to
> get the money but it's hard ... I can't save here ...
> like this week my Mum had no money so I gave her some
> so I've got none now.'

Several other subjects went to live with their parents,
albeit for shorter periods.   One female, for instance,
used her parental home as a place of rest and recupera-
tion.   She spent most of the twelve-month period travelling from place to place, in and out of living-in jobs,
and returned home for the winter, partly to pay off accu-
mulated fines and debts.

> 'I'd like to stick at home and get the fines paid off.
> Then the summer will come and I'll think again ... I'll
> take off again somewhere.'

One problem many subjects faced was that they either
had no parental home to fall back on in emergency or,
where one existed, staying there was made difficult or impossible by conflict with parents or by overcrowding.
This was particularly true of those who came from broken
homes and/or had had 'institutional care' (see chapter 5).
For instance, one female, aged eighteen, said (at the initial interview):   'I'd be living with my father now if it
wasn't for her.'   She was referring to the woman her
father had married after her mother died.
    There was one extreme case of overcrowding, in the case
of a male aged eighteen, who had spent most of his life
since eight in institutions.   At the re-interview he was

temporarily staying with his mother and ten brothers and
sisters in a two-bedroomed council house. The harassed
mother told us that her offspring regularly slept rough
and that she often locked them out.

Many subjects had accommodation problems outside as
well as inside London. One male, for instance, was
having great difficulty finding accommodation in Aberdeen
(at the time we re-interviewed him):

'It's impossible trying to get a place. We went down
to see a flat and there were sixteen other couples
waiting for it, and we had the money right there and we
couldn't get it. There just isn't a chance.... They
want £9 a week for a room and then your electricity
comes on top of that. It's £4 a week for a council
house but that takes about five years.'

He was living in a small rented room (no running water or
inside toilet) with his pregnant wife and they hoped to
get a council flat before the baby was born.

Another man had accommodation problems in Scotland.
He had left for London after a rift with his wife and
children. He blamed the split on bad housing conditions:

'We moved twelve times in one year, it was ridiculous,
how can you live like that ... we had a flat in Paisley
for a few months; we were settled there but then they
built a road through it ... I reckon if we had stayed
there we would still be together.'

He returned to his father's house whereupon his wife
'dumped' the children on him and disappeared:

'I was running up and down to the welfare, but I
couldn't get a house. He [his father] wouldn't let
me keep the kids there any longer so I had to put them
in a home.'

At the time of re-interview his wife had returned and they
were living together again but still in his father's
house.

One female, leaving London after four weeks of homelessness, had little option but to seek accommodation with
her mother. She was already five months pregnant. She
and her boyfriend lived with the mother under great
stress, until (shortly after the baby was born) the situation became intolerable.

'She was going out, I was doing all the work and every-

thing.   Doing all the cooking, minding my brothers,
she says if you don't finish with him [boyfriend] I
want nothing else to do with you.'

Mother threw out the boyfriend after an argument.   She
didn't wish to be separated so she left as well.   They
went to the social services and were housed in an emergency hostel for women and children while the boyfriend
walked the streets.

'It [the hostel] was a terrible place.   It was no
place for a baby.   It was really rough.   It was dis-
gusting really, the carry cot was black, the children
had all different illnesses ... she [the baby] got sick
after two days.   I left and refused to go back.'

The authorities relented and they were all three given a
place in a more acceptable form of homeless family accomo-
dation.
Similar problems were encountered by two other subjects
who met and became lovers while homeless in London.   Just
before their baby was due they returned to the female's
parents and got married.   After the birth the father
threw them out and they went into a homeless families'
hostel.   At re-interview they were anxious about accommodation and angry about the attitude of the social services.

'We've had a lot of trouble with the social services
hanging around ... I know what a social worker is when
I come home from work, she's sitting there performing,
telling me what to do ... I told her in plain English
"Get out."   She ran out like greased lightning ... I
would have knocked the stuffing out of her if she had
gone on any longer....   They were trying to get the
baby away from us.'

'I can't stand them [social workers].   Ninety-nine per
cent of them are a waste of time....'

One response to accommodation problems was squatting,
although this only occurred in London.   Only two males
and one female used this as a long-term solution.   All
three subjects opened up their own squats.   One man was
involved in the squatting movement after being referred to
the Elgin Avenue squats.   His squat was a large elegant
house bordering the canal in Maida Vale.   He lived there
with his wife and new baby in two rooms.   There was heating and lighting and they had basic furniture given to them
by other squatters.   A TV set was given by a neighbour.

The female opened her squat with a friend. She shared
with a homeless family in Kingston:

> 'Me and my friend went down to no. 35. There was a
> board up on the window, we punched it and it fell and
> we climbed in through the toilet window ... we were
> happy there ... some guys came and moved into the up-
> stairs. We were there nine months, it seemed like one
> big family ... I didn't used to go the West End.'

Males

up to 1 week	1–2 weeks	2–4 weeks	4–6 weeks	6–8 weeks	2–4 months	4–6 months	6–9 months	9–12 months
4	6	5	3	2	2	1	1	5

Females

up to 1 week	1–2 weeks	2–4 weeks	4–6 weeks	6–8 weeks	2–4 months	4–6 months	6–9 months	9–12 months
5	2	2		1	1		2	3

FIGURE 8.2 Total length of time homeless (including
squats) in the twelve-month period following the initial
interview (both in London and outside)

Figure 8.2 shows the length of time subjects were
'homeless' (that is, using one or more of the various
types of emergency accommodation specified in Table 8.6)
in the twelve months following the initial interview.
It includes periods outside as well as inside London,
although in most cases homelessness was restricted to
London. Table 8.6 gives the main type of emergency
accommodation used over this period, according to the
total length of time 'homeless'. In some cases subjects
used a wide range of types.

EMPLOYMENT

Table 8.7 shows the employed status of the follow-up
sample twelve months after the initial interview relative
to that at the time of deciding to leave the last settled
base. Table 8.9 shows that a large majority spent most
of the year unemployed. Fifteen males (52 per cent) and
seven females (44 per cent) had worked for less than one

TABLE 8.6 Main type of emergency accommodation used by follow-up sample while homeless in the twelve-month period following the initial interview (according to total length of time homeless during this period)

Type of accommodation	Males				Females			
	Length of time homeless				Length of time homeless			
	Up to one month	One to four months	Four to twelve months	Total	Up to one month	One to four months	Four to twelve months	Total
Emergency hostels	4	–	–	4	7	–	–	7
Squats	1	3	3	7	–	1	1	2
Reception centres	5	1	–	6	–	–	–	–
Sleeping rough	4	1	–	5	–	–	–	–
Staying with friends	1	–	–	1	2	1	–	3
Short-term hostels	–	2	1	3	–	–	2	2
Homeless family hostels	–	–	1	1	–	–	2	2
Lodging houses	–	–	2	2	–	–	–	–
Total	15	7	7	29	9	2	5	16

TABLE 8.7 Employment status twelve months after initial interview relative to that at time of deciding to leave LSB

Employment status as at time of deciding to leave LSB	Employment status twelve months after initial interview			
	Employed	Unemployed	Prison	Total
Males:				
Employed	3	2	1	6
Unemployed	5	8	5	18
Inactive (school or institution)	2	1	-	3
No LSB since leaving prison	-	1	1	2
Total	10	12	7	29
Females:				
Employed	-	2	-	2
Unemployed	3	7	-	10
Inactive (school or institution)	3	-	-	4
No LSB since leaving prison	-	-	-	-
Total	6	10	-	16

month, and only three males and three females had worked for over nine months. With the exception of one subject work was unskilled or semi-skilled.

TABLE 8.8 Main means of support during twelve-month period following initial interview

Means of support	Males	Females
Employment	8	7
Unemployment and/or supplementary benefit	8	8
Institutions and probation hostels	9	-
Crime	3	-
Prostitution	1	-
Parents/relatives	-	1
Total	29	16

TABLE 8.9 Employment record in the twelve-month period following initial interview relative to employment status at time of leaving last settled base

Employment status at time of deciding to leave LSB	No work	Under one month	One to three months	Three to six months	Six to nine months	Nine to twelve months	Total
Males:							
Employed	1	2	–	–	1	2	6
Unemployed	4	5	3	3	2	1	18
Inactive	1	–	–	–	2	–	3
No LSB since leaving prison	2	–	–	–	–	–	2
Total	8	7	3	3	5	3	29
Females:							
Employed	1	1	–	–	–	–	2
Unemployed	1	4	2	1	–	2	10
Inactive	–	–	–	2	1	1	4
Total	2	5	2	3	1	3	16

Number of months' employment

DEVIANCE

Criminal processing since initial interview compared with
that before it

Table 8.10 shows the incidence of criminal processing both
before and after the first interview.   In addition, four
males and one female traced had been through the courts.
The female was fined.   One male had received a prison
sentence and the three others supervision sentences.   One
of those placed on probation had no previous criminal
record.   Of the twenty men (both re-interviews and
traces) receiving sentences subsequent to the initial
interview, eight received one or more sentences while
homeless in London.

Psychiatric processing

The proportion of our whole sample receiving psychiatric
treatment prior to the initial interview was 19 per cent
of males and 14 per cent of females compared to 24 per
cent (seven) of males and 31 per cent (five) of females in
the follow-up sample.   The females who had had prior
treatment (three as in-patients; two as out-patients) had
had no subsequent treatment in the twelve-month period
following the first interview.   Four males had had further treatment, all as in-patients.   A further male who
had been an out-patient was receiving psychotherapy and
drug treatment in prison.
    One male who had absconded from compulsory mental hos-
pital treatment in Scotland returned to it.   There he remained for ten months, three months longer than necessary
because of the difficulty in finding accommodation for
himself and his pregnant wife.   He was doubtful whether
the treatment was effective:

    'These places never do me any good.   I can do better
    myself.   I proved this last time I was in.... They
    always give me drugs but I never take them, I just
    throw them away ... I suppose at times drugs are OK but
    you get to a point where they make you feel worse and
    worse.'

Drugs

At the initial interview, ten males and one female admitted to being current regular users of the 'harder' kind of

TABLE 8.10 Criminal processing since initial interview compared with that before it

First interview criminal record	Criminal processing since first interview				
	None	Minor	Supervision	Custodial	Total
Males:					
None	3	1	–	1	5
Minor	4	1	1	–	6
Supervision	2	–	–	1	3
Custodial	4	1	3	7	15
Total	13	3	4	9	29
Females:					
None	8	–	3	–	11
Minor	2	–	–	–	2
Supervision	2	–	1	–	3
Custodial	–	–	–	–	–
Total	12	0	4	0	16

drugs (including narcotics, amphetamines, barbiturates and LSD, but excluding hashish).   Seven of these (six males and one female) appeared again in the follow-up sample. Four males and one female had been regular barbiturate or amphetamine users and of these two males and the female were still regularly using these drugs.   She had had three convictions for possession of drugs.   One of those males for whom these drugs had been a problem claimed to be off them and using only hashish and occasional LSD. However he was convicted for possession of barbiturates, for which he received a Borstal sentence.   Another male had been and still was a heroin addict. The final male who had been a current regular user of LSD was still using it.

A second group were those using drugs only occasionally at the first interview or who had subsequently become users.   One female using amphetamines occasionally at the first interview was on amphetamines and barbiturates regularly twelve months later.   She was living in the West End with addicts and prostitutes and obtaining drugs regularly from friends.   She subsequently gave up after a friend died from an overdose.

A female we traced had no experience of drugs at the initial interview but took to regular use of barbiturates while in London.   A friend of hers said she was a heavy user combining them with alcohol.   Initially she had begun 'for kicks' and later used them regularly to 'go through with prostitution'.

Two females who had taken LSD occasionally, no longer took drugs of any kind.   Two males and the female who had not taken LSD before took some occasionally while living in London but not after leaving.

Two males and one female made a living from selling drugs.   One male and the female were importing drugs in small quantities and made several trips abroad.   We also know that one man traced who was selling hard drugs at his first interview was thrown out of his probation hostel for buying narcotics.

Alcohol abuse

At the time of the initial interview thirteen males and two females in the whole sample acknowledged that their drinking was currently a problem (i.e.in the last six months before interview) and five males acknowledged past difficulties: ten of these males and one female appeared again in the follow-up sample.

All but two males said they had had no further difficulties with drink since the first interview.   Four of the ten spent the greater part of the year in prison and presumably without access to drink.

However, being in an institution did not necessarily mean no access to alcohol.   One male, also with a current problem at the time of the first interview, told us how he was frequently drunk in psychiatric hospital.   The other male who had further problems believed he became 'virtually an alcoholic'.   He had spent a lot of time homeless 'mixing with junkies and alcoholics'.

One male who had been merely a social drinker now felt he had a problem.   At the time of re-interview he was on three charges directly related to drink and had had two convictions for being drunk and disorderly.   He had also been sacked from a job as a barman for drinking.

Attempted suicides

We found that three males and two females in the follow-up sample had attempted suicide or endangered their lives subsequent to the first interview.   Of these one male had previously made a suicide attempt.   One female and a male attempted suicide while homeless in London.   The male confessed to feigning it to get a bed and food.   He had a life-saving certificate and jumped off a bridge a few yards from a police launch.

CHILD-BEARING AND CHANGES IN MARITAL STATUS

Three males and two females married in the twelve-month intervening period.   One of these males married one of the females.   The other female married an immigrant for money.   One male estranged from his wife and children at the time of the first interview later returned to them.

Four female subjects gave birth in the twelve-month period - one in a Cairo hotel room whilst travelling, with her husband, around the world.   The wife of a male sample member gave birth to a further child.   One male subject fathered three children (including twins) and had no plans for marrying.

The responsibility of marriage and children was highly valued as giving a reason to settle:

'When we were in London I was free to go where I like, do what I like, but that life was not good for me. You need security.   Somewhere you can turn back to. I went from pillar to post.   I was touch enough to take it so I took it ... my life's come to a halt now I

can't do what I want.   Marriage means responsibility,
that's what you get married for.'

A female had expressed the wish for a child at the
first interview:

'What did I say to you when you saw me?   I said that
all I wanted was a little child, wasn't it?   Well now
I've done it.   I said I would ... I only stay here
because of her, well you can't go gadding about the
place with a small baby.'

IMPROVEMENT OR DETERIORATION?

Here we ask the general question: had the situations of
our subjects taken as a group improved or deteriorated by
the end of the twelve months following the initial interview?   This is a difficult question since it depends on
what (or rather whose) standards we adopt.   Not all our
subjects shared the conventional view.   For instance, one
male said:

'What is there to settle down for?   I like to keep
moving.'

However, most subjects accepted that being settled, having
a job and living in comfortable, preferably independent,
accommodation were desirable states if the price to pay
was not too high.
      On these scores, there may have been, on balance, a
marginal improvement, compared to their situation in their
LSB prior to coming to London.   There was a net increase
of four males and four females in employment, although
this was mostly accounted for by two males and three
females becoming employed who had been previously ineligible for work (through being at school or in an institution).   On the other hand, five males had left the dole
queue for prison.   As regards accommodation, there was a
net reduction of six males and four females dependent on
parents, relatives or friends and a net increase of five
males and three females living in their own rented accommodation, squats and lodgings or having living-in jobs.
However, the price paid for being less dependent on
parents, etc. for accommodation was sometimes less comfort
or security.   On the other hand, there was a net increase
of five males in prison (if we take into account the two
males whose LSB was effectively prison) although this was
partly compensated for by a net reduction of three males

in other institutional settings.   The number of females
homeless had increased from one to four.   However, two of
the latter were living with their partners in homeless
family units and were in line for council flats.

However, orthodox material indices of well being are
not necessarily a guide to feelings about self and their
whole situation.   Indications as to our subjects' psychological states in their LSB came through the initial
interview.   At this time, they were liable to be disor-
iented by their precipitation into an unfamiliar, uncertain situation, by the pressures of destitution and by the
absence of usual constraints and supports.   They were
living at emotional extremes in an extreme situation.   It
is not surprising then that they often appeared to be
anxious, depressed, pre-occupied, guarded or confused, or
alternatively 'up and down', excitable, unrealistically
optimistic or prone to invent and experiment with new
identities.   At the follow-up interview they seemed more
grounded, relaxed, coherent and 'balanced'.   This change
probably reflected the fact that we were interviewing them
on their own territory, by appointment and at a much less
stressful (or less expansive) time in their lives.

At the re-interview, subjects seemed more accepting (or
resigned) towards their situation than the one that led
them to leave their LSB.   This partly reflected the fact
that we were less likely to interview than just after a
critical or fluid situation, similar to the one that had
prompted them to come to London.   However, some subjects
had partly become more reconciled to their situation as a
result of having been to London.   Relative to being homeless in London, their current, usually more settled state
usually seemed a better bet.   As one male, reunited with
his wife and children, said:

> 'I'd be stupid to go back.   I'd only go back for a
> holiday or if I had a good job to go to ... I had
> enough last time.'

There was often a feeling that they had learned a
lesson or got something out of their system.   A few even
felt they were transformed.   For instance, in her initial
interview one fifteen-year-old girl talked about being 'a
bit of a wild one' and of the 'rough' friends she had who
took drugs, lived in squats and got into trouble with the
police.   She described numerous conflicts with her
parents that had prompted her to run away to London.   At
the re-interview, she seemed demure and embarrassed by her
previous rebelliousness.   She was living harmoniously
with her parents and had rejected her previous friends:

'I've changed a lot since then ... I'm on a higher
level.   I don't mix with people like that anymore.'

Like this girl, several subjects had changed their
definition of well being.   This applied particularly to
one sixteen-year-old girl, an exceptionally articulate
and introspective subject.   In her LSB she had been
living in a Young People's Psychiatric Unit.   At the
first interview she said she had been happy in London but
now assessed the situation differently:

'I was happy in London in the sense of floating around
on cloud nine.   It was a false happiness.   More a
relief to be away from teachers, parents, law, authority, doctors, ... I'm a lot happier than a year ago,
now I get on with living.   Then I was much more inside
myself and more in tune with myself even though I
didn't understand myself....   Now I'm further away
from me, but I'm glad to be away from me.   Me is a
bottomless pit of emotions.   Now I'm sticking to a wee
cold room up on top otherwise I get lost ... the
living-in job pulled me out of the pit, but now I
wonder what's going on there.'

She had become much less rebellious, but as she herself
acknowledged, had lost something in terms of vitality.
She had sacrificed the highs to avoid the downs.
Many subjects found comparisons between then and now
not very relevant.   There was still a strong theme of
living for the present moment.   Living in the present
sometimes meant not thinking about the past experience in
London:

'I don't think about it ... I just think it wasn't a
nice time.   I remember the things I've done when I
think about it ... I think about what I did to other
people not really what happened to me.   I don't think
about it, because it's not interesting ... I want to
get on terms with myself.   I want to grow up.'
(female)

But, as we have shown, London was not usually an exclusively negative experience.   For a few subjects at
least, their time in London had been on balance a positive
one.   For one male in particular, the risk taken in
coming to London had more than paid off.   After a rough
time to begin with, he had managed to settle there with
his girlfriend:

'Everything is very rosy now: I've got a good job (as
assistant sales manager), we've got a flat and we've
got money in the bank.   We'd like to stay here for
ever and ever.'

Chapter 9

CONCLUSION

Our study, largely researched between 1974 and 1976, has
considerable limitations. Especially in chapter 3 we
have indicated what some of these are. Our sample is not
representative of any clearly definable population. It
was selected from among the users of three projects,
chosen somewhat arbitrarily and in no way representative
of the general provision for homeless young newcomers.
Our decision to lump together the sample quotas from each
of these projects is questionable given differences in the
types of young people they tend to attract. The longer
individuals stayed (or were allowed to stay) in these projects, the more likely they were to be represented in our
sample. We only managed to follow up and re-interview
40 per cent of the male subjects and 46 per cent of the
females. We have focused rather more on the colour of
individual experience than on the large-scale features of
structure and social administration. Our research is
passing into history. Agencies in homelessness are constantly changing - some no longer exist and others referred to, including the West End Reception Centre (WERC) and
Centrepoint, have altered substantially since 1976.
    An important restriction is that we examined only a
small segment of that whole area which, by various definitions, is described as homelessness. We have not looked
at the indigenous homeless, those coming from the Greater
London Council area; we have not looked at the long-term
homeless, thoroughly settled into the Piccadilly scene or
others even outside the West End. We have given little
attention to crashpadding or sleeping rough or to the
older homeless population who have already been well researched. (1) This book has been centrally about those
young migrants from the provinces to London, some of whom,
whilst still fresh to homelessness there, were admitted
into one of our three selected projects - Centrepoint,

185

WERC and the now defunct North.   We have not looked at
young migrants who did not use those projects, perhaps
using others in and outside the central area.

So this study necessarily presents a limited view of
the whole situation.   Just as the various agencies suffer
from what we have described as the 'snapshot effect' -
seeing clients only in relation to their own provision and
contact and having little information about those returning home or obtaining private accommodation (in some ways
the 'successes') - so in some respects does our research.
The clients tell stories to researchers as well as to the
agencies and full validation has not usually been possible.   We know little of the points of view of the various people mentioned by subjects: their parents whom some
accused of being unreasonable;   the people who worked in
the wide range of social agencies and institutions, with
which they had contact;   and in particular, the staff of
the agencies they used while homeless in London, some of
whom were severely criticised.

Our major interest has been in the consumer.   How does
he or she see the world?   That has meant that we have
taken sometimes a simplistic view of the way the agencies
operate.   We have not always fully understood their particular problems and policies.   However, we would justify
that bias by saying that consumers contribute little to
the formulation of policies by either statutory bodies or
voluntary societies.

Consumers, agencies and ourselves are strongly influenced by immense social currents;   sometimes swept along
by them.   These currents include the prevailing and
rapidly changing ideologies outlined in chapter 4, with
their implications for the way in which young people, especially homeless ones, are perceived and responded to.
They also include structural changes in accommodation,
employment and mobility, which are also inextricably
linked to the fate of the young homeless.   An added
dimension is the role played by any social processing
undergone before they become homeless.

Accommodation: it is increasingly difficult for young
people to find reasonable housing.   Various sorts of
accommodation in London and other cities, like lodging
houses and hostels, have been gradually disappearing
largely because of inner city redevelopment programmes.
The vast majority of single adults have no home of their
own, relying on either parents or lodgings.   Where individuals have no real home, like those leaving children's
institutions, they can run into serious difficulties as we
have seen from this study.   Young homeless people usually
have little access to the two major sources of housing -
home ownership or the public rented sector.

The Housing (Homeless Persons) Act, 1977, seems to have
been reasonably successful with the accommodation of families. (2)   The Act, however, places no particular mandatory responsibility on local authorities to provide for
the young.   The priority categories for accommodation are
pregnancy, having dependent children, being homeless as a
result of an emergency and being otherwise vulnerable, to
include old age, mental illness or handicap or other
special reasons.   This latter category may include persons at risk because of their youth.
    Our study gives grounds for concern about housing pro-
vision for young people.   While in London, few of the
sample obtained accommodation, for any length of time,
outside the homeless circuit.   Nationally, there was a
gain in single households of 98 per cent and in flat-shar-
ing of 74 per cent among those aged twenty to twenty-five
years in the period 1966-71, with no great increase in the
total numbers in that age range. (3)   If this increase
continues, it must put even greater pressure on the pro-
portionately small stock of suitable accommodation.
    Within the existing legislation, particularly under the
Housing Finance Act, 1974 (establishment of the Housing
Corporation and various special financial arrangements)
there is considerable scope for the development of lodgings schemes, flatlets, hostels and bed-sit provision, all
playing a role in accommodating the young homeless. (4)
However, there must be a strong case for amending the 1977
Act to include mandatory provision by local authorities
for the young homeless.
    Employment: changes in the labour market are another
important dimension - one linked to that of accommodation.
The proportion of unemployed under twenty-five years increased both during and after the period of our study.
Department of Employment figures indicate that in July
1973, 23 per cent of the males and 51 per cent of females
unemployed were under twenty-five.   By July 1974 that
proportion had increased to 26 per cent for males and 55
per cent for females.   July 1976 saw a further increase
to 36 per cent for males and 65 per cent for females. (5)
At that time, the unemployment rate for those under
twenty-five was 8.75 per cent compared with a rate of 4.3
per cent for those over twenty-five years old. (6)
    In an economic recession, young people are more vulner-
able to unemployment.   Many cannot get started in work;
some may be sacked earlier because they create fewer redundancy payment problems.   Apprentices may be asked to
leave at eighteen years old because wages must be increased by law.   Young people are more mobile so considerable numbers leave jobs voluntarily and move elsewhere.

Most of the sample were unable to get reasonably paid work.   Many came from areas of relatively high unemploy-ment and had been unemployed already when leaving their last settled base.   The vast majority had few educational or occupational qualifications to assist in an increasing-ly competitive labour market.   When they found work, it was mainly casual and in industries like catering where both wages and employment conditions were poor.

However, there is a tendency to oversimplify the link between unemployment and homelessness.   It is clear that many young people leave their last settled base for reasons other than lack of work.   They are seeking ex-citement and a change of scene.   Even where unemployment is a major motive, it is usually mixed with others.   No one has managed to explain the discrepancy between the high proportion of young Scots among the users of Centre-point and WERC and the relatively low proportions from other areas of high unemployment such as Northern England and Wales.   Further, if unemployment were directly signi-ficant, we might have expected a significant and sustained increase in the number of homeless young newcomers between 1974 and 1978, a period over which unemployment has been rising considerably.   No such increase has been recorded by the homeless agencies.

There is a considerable future for comprehensive schemes which combine work and accommodation.   In partic-ular, Manpower Services Commission (MSC) programmes offer a number of possibilities for employing young people in large cities and elsewhere.   Some educational and train-ing programmes, particularly those pioneered by Kingsway College, offer a flexible curriculum aimed at disadvan-taged youngsters.

Mobility: one major theme of our study has been the movement of young people into London and away from their last settled base.   Most of our subjects moved distances of over 200 miles.   Increasing numbers of young people, as we have seen from the growth in single-person house-holds, want to leave home before getting married and having children.   This coincides with serious accommoda-tion shortages especially in the privately rented sector.

Robins and Cohen suggest that there are considerable class differences in mobility patterns. (7)

The assertion of youthful independence conforms to the fundamental class divide.   On one side, those who em-brace studenthood, accept wageless dependence, on their families or State grants, and whose struggle is for a place of their own to be who they like in.   On the other, those who take for granted the fact of continued

domestic dependence, because their target is a wage of
their own to do what they like with.

Our sample seem to be searching for both space and adequate money.   They leave their last settled base often in
the most unpremeditated and unprepared way.   However,
attitudes towards the struggle for independence among
these young people are viewed quite differently from the
middle classes.   Leaving home to become a student or a
nurse is valued whereas 'running away to sea/London' is
viewed as evading family and other responsibilities.

In subtle ways, the homeless agencies can reflect those
wider processes of stigmatisation.   After Six's poster/
leaflet campaign 'Don't come to London' not only shows a
Canute-like determination in the face of major social
forces but may also reflect a view that many young people
ought not to be coming anyway.   The Pavlovian tendency of
Camden social workers to return young people to their
homes with little thought of the conditions there, might
reflect a similar tendency.   Dire warnings as to the terrible conditions in Soho and elsewhere such as those contained in 'Johnny Go Home' might be counterproductive in
some cases.   Those youngsters seeking a 'devilish time'
would be positively attracted by the warnings.

However, the whole question of where to intervene has
increasingly concerned the agencies in the West End since
New Horizon began its Glasgow work in the 1970-1 period.
Most of the sample had had contacts with an assortment of
agencies in their last settled base and their presence in
London is partly a reflection of the lack of facilities in
the home towns.   There is clearly a case for more extensive services for young people, including all kinds of
accommodation, crisis centres and detached youth work. (8)

To a large extent, the young people in the sample were
already tangled up in a network of social processing.
Fifty per cent of the males and 34 per cent of the females
had spent some time in an 'institution' before the initial
interview.   Of these, the majority had been in community
homes (or equivalents), but, in the case of the males,
well over half had already graduated on to criminal and
psychiatric institutions (see chapter 5).   At least eight
males (11 per cent) left their last settled base mainly to
escape processing in criminal, psychiatric or child-care
settings.   A further seven males, three of them also
evading processing, had had no settled base since leaving
prison.

Some tended to survive the difficult situation in
London partly through various street crimes; picking
pockets, prostitution and mugging.   One major social ele-

ment was the number who were (or recently had been) concerned about their own alcohol consumption.   Eighteen
males and two females admitted to difficulties with drinking.   Their drifting street life generally makes them an
easy target for the police and other agencies.   Their
deviance is easily visible. (9)

Some existing facilities seem to make a negative impact
on these young people.   They complained about lack of
sympathetic treatment from psychiatric services, social
security offices and some homeless agencies, amongst
others.   They felt treated as children, 'social lepers'
and as 'malingerers'.   Traditional services probably need
better access points for these young people.   The development of the Walk-In medical centre in the West End and
also information and advice facilities are particularly
good examples of this.

One important aspect of our research has been the construction of ideological models which relate to positions
taken by the agencies and observers of the homeless scene.
These models are crude but illuminate major influences in
forming priorities and policies.   They form frameworks by
which agencies draw almost Poor Law style distinctions between the 'deserving' and the 'undeserving'.

The five models illustrated in chapter 4 - individual
culpability, political, religious, pathological and child
- represent clusters of attitudes rarely found unadultera-
ted in the homeless literature.   The individual culpability model simply holds homeless people responsible for
their own condition and so 'undeserving'.   Strong echoes
of the 1834 Poor Law Amendment Act.

We want to make things difficult for the homeless by
putting them into a hostel (Richard Badcock, Cornish
councillor, October 1978 and quoted in the CHAR news-
letter Nov./Dec. 1978).

Ron Bailey gives us a typical broadside with the political model and interestingly implies that personal problems are traceable to various forms of poor policy-making
and council and central government decisions.

Because of the years of total neglect of the problem
(homelessness) by local authorities, because of the
lack of secure accommodation, social services help and
secure employment, and often because of family break-
ups, the single homeless often have other problems too,
which lack of accommodation only exacerbates ('The
Homeless and the Empty Houses', Penguin, 1977, p. 52).

Eileen Eisenklam of GALS gives an example of the child model:

> We counselled in the belief that a young person would take responsibility and accept the consequences for her own actions. But this was often at variance with the expectations of the clients whose ignorance of the facts of life left them frequently unfit to take mature decisions.(Young Girls alone in London, 'Social Work Today', 10. 10. 78)

Whereas the child model blossoms in popularity, it is increasingly difficult to locate recent examples of the religious and pathological models. As Peter Archard comments, 'Traditional moral indignation is transformed into the language of contemporary humanism.' (10)   However some whiffs of latter-day evangelism emerge from the cosmetic of modern descriptions.

> The aim of this service will be a reversal of the drift towards self destruction characterising rootless existence in the area [West End] ('West End Co-ordinated Voluntary Services,Submission for Urban Aid', 1974, p. 37).

More commonly, statements are a hybridisation of different perceptions. This passage is from the foreword to the 1977 'Centrepoint Report' and contains echoes of political and pathological factors ending with the child model.

> They [workers in homeless agencies] have to contend with the social and economic problems resulting from prolonged and mounting inflation and stubbornly high unemployment. Those who seek accommodation for the night have their own difficulties. It may be a family relationship that has gone wrong, or some deep disappointment of their hopes. There may be ill-health, physical or mental. Frequently, for whatever cause, there is a failure to relate realistically and practically to what can seem a bewildering and frustrating world.

Our study indicates that few subjects identify with the ideologies of the homeless agencies. The agencies monopolise the public discussion and definition of the phenomenon which leads directly to a neglect of the consumer's standpoint. Such ideologies can be simply expedient: aspects of the survival needs of the agencies to attain

increased influence and to expand.   Consequently the
phenomenon of homeless young people, and particularly its
media presentation, is distorted, simplified and drama-
tised.   The homeless are presented as more hapless and
hopeless than our study would indicate.

Whereas the views of the projects are often uncomplica-
ted and dogmatic, the perceptions of consumers are complex
and continually shifting.   The annual reports and campaign documents of the voluntary societies stress their
own centrality in efforts to 'solve' homelessness.
Apparently, without their work in counselling and residential provision, young people would drift wholesale into
petty crime, prostitution and mental illness.   That
belief in their own importance is not borne out by this
study.   Informal networks, grapevines, squatting and
sleeping rough play a much larger part, at least quantita-
tively, in the homeless experiences of these young people.

The importance of the models is that they imply different 'solutions'.   Political models prescribe large-scale
social and economic changes, particularly in housing and
employment.   The pathological model restricts the problem
to a smaller number of young people who are 'sick' and requiring various kinds of treatment.   It seeks specific
individualised and localised solutions rather than major
social intervention.   There is a perceived need for
social work, psychotherapy and counselling to treat emotional deprivation.   Movements in ideology, like Centrepoint's from the political to the pathological during
1972-6, may reflect increased difficulties in structural
intervention than any real change in the nature of young
people's problems.

So long as agencies claim that homeless young people
are a special case, they can also claim special resources.
If these youngsters become the 'tip of the iceberg' then
huge resources are required to spread thinly over a wide
population.   To qualify for the 'special case' help,
they must be seen as disabled and no help can be available for them in the various intermediate stages.   Energy
is focused on the homeless but not on the same people at
potentially more fruitful periods of their existence, for
example, struggling to survive in a bed-sitter or flat.

One important area lies in exploring the possibility of
more diffusive institutions like the defunct North - institutions which are less formal and less concerned with
their own self-maintenance.   When the Mexican campesino
migrates, he normally follows an itinerary laid down by
relatives and friends.   They provide him with an informal
network of contacts, including initial housing, information and advice and even an informal labour exchange. (11)

Very few of our sample had any contacts in London, so such help has to be provided by the community. We need services which can easily refer outwards to squats and privately rented accommodation rather than become involved in the incestuous process of referring further along the homeless circuit. Such services could have a greater respect for self-help capacities.

That respect can grow from a greater understanding of the adventure and survival themes in the journey of these young people. For the majority of the sample, the journey to London is the start of an adventure which could end in triumph or disaster. They are taking an enormous risk.

Their whole 'here-and-now' approach, which the agencies find so frustrating, can actually be an aid to surviving. 'Here-and-now' may be vital in coping with much hardship and deprivation. It may echo the process outlined in Alexander Solhenitzyn's 'One Day in the Life of ...'. It may become a necessary way of excluding, at least for the present, a potentially bleak future by simply concentrating on the immediate - the next bed, the next meal. This means a rejection of the heavy philosophy of deferred gratification and planning which most agencies stress in their intervention.

Being homeless is one possible consequence of trying to change homes and establish independence. Youth is a time for exploring and taking risks before eventually settling down. Some youngsters have been using us and the projects to explore different identities, different ways of living and being. Those efforts deserve respect. The former Voluntary Hostels Conference (later National Association for Voluntary Hostels) experimented in using an eighteen-year-old Scottish police cadet. This strapping lad was to sleep on the homeless circuit for two weeks and produce a report. After several nights homeless in central London, he had reached such a pitch of physical exhaustion and personal depression that the experiment had to end. (12)

Many survivors in this book lived out for weeks and months in central London. They showed considerable courage and resourcefulness, in contrast to the sickly and helpless portraits frequently sketched by the project reports. In other settings, these young people would have merited the Duke of Edinburgh's gold award or achieved a single-handed Atlantic crossing.

Their imagination and adventure is met by the hard practical edge of social service provision intent in offering a number of packages, many of them thoroughly evangelical in nature. We become ever more technological

in our approach to human problems.   This increasingly
popular engineering approach denies the imagination and
meaning in people's lives.   Peter Berger puts it most
succinctly: (13)

> In principle, there is an assumption that all human
> problems can be converted into technical problems, and
> if the techniques to solve certain problems do not yet
> exist, then they will have to be invented.   The world
> becomes ever more 'makeable'.

NOTES

CHAPTER 1   HOMELESS YOUNG PEOPLE

1   Kellow Chesney, 'The Victorian Underworld', Penguin,
    1972, pp. 424-5 and 240-2.
2   Edwin Hodder, 'The Life and Work of the Seventh Earl
    of Shaftesbury K.G.', Cassell, 1893, p. 399.
3   Ibid., p. 400.
4   Sidney Webb, 'English Poor Law History: Part 2 - The
    Last Hundred Years', Longmans Green & Co Ltd, 1927.
5   C.L. Mowatt, 'The Charity Organisation Society 1869-
    1913', Methuen, 1961.
6   Charles Booth, 'Life and Labour of the People in
    London', Vol. 1, Macmillan, 1892, p. 233.
7   'Charity Organisation Society Review', 1881, Vol. X,
    p. 50.
8   Octavia Hill, 'Homes of the London Poor', Macmillan,
    1884, p. 10.
9   Frank Gray, 'The Tramp - His Meaning and Being', Dent,
    1931, p. 55.   See also Report to the Ministry of
    Health of the Departmental Committee on the Relief of
    the Casual Poor, presented July 1930, Cmd 3640, HMSO.
    The appendix by Dr E.O. Lewis sketches out a
    whole area of pathology in vagrancy.   Of 592 casual
    poor examined - 15.7 per cent were feeble minded;
    5.4 per cent insane;   5.7 per cent psychoneurotic;
    12.3 per cent chronic alcoholic.
10 Frank Gray, 'The Tramp - His Meaning and Being', p.
    58.
11 Anton Wallich-Clifford, 'Caring on Skid Row', Veritas,
    1976, p. 11.
12 Stuart Whiteley, Down and Out in London - Mental Ill-
    ness in the Lower Social Groups, 'The Lancet', 17
    September 1955.
13 Howard Bahr, 'The Disaffiliated Man', Oxford Univer-
    sity Press, 1973, pp. 120-1.

14 New Horizon Annual Report, 1974.
15 Ibid., 1975-6, p. 3.
16 Gillian Diamond, 'Homelessness', paper given to the National Association of Youth Clubs, 2 October 1974.
17 Margaret Norris, 'Report on Single Homelessness in Surrey', Surrey Community Development Trust, 1974, p. 7.
18 Theodore Caplow, 'Homelessness', ed. David Sills, International Encyclopedia of the Social Sciences. Quoted in Howard Bahr's 'The Disaffiliated Man', Macmillan, New York, 1968, p. 17, Vol. 6, pp. 494-9.
19 Peter Beresford, Problems of Homelessness, 'Social Services Quarterly', Winter 1974-5, pp. 263-4.
20 Department of the Environment and Department of Health and Social Security, 'Homelessness', Circular 18/74, 7 February 1974.
21 Rosamunde Blackler and Eileen Eisenklam, London's Homeless Girls, 'New Society', 6 May 1976.
22 Barbara Ward, 'The Home of Man', Penguin, 1976, p. 116.
23 See for example David Brandon, 'Homeless in London', Christian Action, 1971; Pamela Page, Camberwell Reception Centre, 'New Society', 22 April 1965.
24 Gillian Diamond, 'Alone with no Home', After Six, 1972.
25 David Eversley, Are we better housed?, 'New Society', 14 April 1977.
26 Jane Morton, Who'll house the single?, 'New Society', 25 March 1976.
27 Peter Wingfield Digby, 'Hostels and Lodgings for Single People', HMSO, 1976, p. 31.
28 Robin Pedley, Students go home, 'Education Guardian', 17 December 1974.
29 'Evening Standard', 15 January 1975.
30 Jane Morton, Who'll house the single?
31 Department of the Environment, 'Housing Single People 1', HMSO, 1971.
32 Joan Clegg, 'Problems in housing policy', British Association of Social Workers, 1975, p. 4.
33 Greater London Council, London Boroughs' Association, 'Working Party on the Provision of Accommodation for Single People: Interim Report', April 1975.
34 Ruth Rooney and Rachel Woolf, 'Claimant to be Doubted?', Grassmarket Project, 1975.
35 Barbara Ward, 'The Home of Man', p. 40.
36 John Hughes, Employ the young, 'New Society', 14 October 1976.
37 Joanna Mack, Youth out of work, 'New Society', 21 April 1977.

38   Marie Brown and Andrew Erlam, 'Catering for Homeless
     Workers', CHAR, 1976.
39   Community Relations Commission, 'Unemployment and
     Homelessness', HMSO, 1974.
40   'Youth Unemployment: Causes and Cures', British Youth
     Council, 1976.
41   Anne Davies, 'The Provision of Medical Care for the
     Homeless and Rootless', CHAR, 1975.
42   Liverpool Community Health Council, 'Medical Care of
     the Single Homeless', February 1977.
43   Peter Wingfield Digby, 'Hostels and Lodgings for
     Single People', pp. 190-1.
44   Joy Holloway, 'They can't fit in', National Council
     of Social Service, 1970.
45   Howard Bahr, 'The Disaffiliated Man', p. 44.

CHAPTER 2   THE HOMELESS SCENE

1   See for example David Brandon, 'Homeless in London',
    Christian Action, 1971; David Tidmarsh, Psychiatric
    Aspects of Destitution, in John Wing, ed., 'Evaluating
    a Community Mental Health Service', Oxford University
    Press, 1972.
2   David Brandon, 'Euston Project - The End of the Line',
    Christian Action, 1974; Roy Walmsley, 'Steps from
    Prison', Regional Group Consultative Committee for
    After Care Hostels, 1972: 'Fifty-five per cent of
    discharged prisoners are quite possibly homeless.'
    See for example Home Office, 'Working Party on Vagran-
    cy and Street Offences', December 1974: which sug-
    gests the retention of a reframed form of the vagrancy
    offences in causing a nuisance by sleeping rough,
    begging, being found on enclosed premises and suspec-
    ted persons.
3   Peter Wingfield Digby, 'Hostels and Lodgings for
    Single People', HMSO, 1976 (see section on quality of
    accommodation).
4   Ibid., p. 31.
5   Ibid., p. 38.
6   Ibid., p. 127.
7   National Assistance Board, 'Reception Centres for per-
    sons without a settled way of living', HMSO, 1952;
    Peter Beresford, Reception Centres: an index of
    social service inadequacy, 'British Journal of Social
    Work', 5.2.
8   David Brandon, Homeless single persons, 'British
    Journal of Psychiatric Social Work', December 1969.
9   Joint Circular of the Department of the Environment

and the Department of Health and Social Services,
Circular 18/74, 'Homelessness', 7 February 1974;
Department of Health and London Boroughs' Association,
'Final report of the joint Working Party on Homeless-
ness in London', 26 June 1972.

10 CHAR, 'Annual Report 1976-77': CHAR adopted a policy
that young people should be included as a priority
group in the Housing Bill 1977.

11 Medical centre for homeless, The 'Guardian', 10
October 1977.

12 Roy Walmsley, 'Steps from Prison'; Stuart Whiteley,
Down and Out in London - mental illness in the lower
social groups, The 'Lancet', 17 September 1955.

13 William Booth, 'Darkest England and the Way Out',
Salvation Army, 1890.

14 Anton Wallich-Clifford, 'Simon Scene', Simon Community, 1969.

15 Chris Blackwell, 'Cyrenian Principles', The Cyrenians,
1973.

16 St Mungos have been involved in a very extensive research project with the Institute of Social Psychiatry
at the Maudsley Hospital.

17 Soho Project, 'Annual Reports'.

18 Department of Health and Social Security, 'Working
Group on Homeless Young People', July 1976, Appendix
1 - The Gleave Case.

19 Blenheim Project, 'People Adrift', April 1974.

20 Marie Keegan et al., 'The Problems of Irish Youth in
London', Benburb Base, 1971.

21 Irish Centre, 'Annual Report', 1971.

22 West End Co-ordinated Voluntary Services, 'Young Scots
in London', The Scots Group, 1976.

23 Girls in London Service (GALS), Annual Reports.

24 Campaign for the Homeless and Rootless (CHAR), Annual
Reports.

25 Charles Booth, 'Life and Labour of the People in
London', Vol. 1, Macmillan, 1892, p. 206.

26 Peter Wingfield Digby, 'Hostels and Lodgings for
Single People', p. 33.

27 Peter Beresford, The Caff - last refuge for the homeless, 'Community Care', 14 July 1976.

28 NAVH - was then called Voluntary Hostels Conference;
see 'Sunday Times', 30 September 1962.

29 National Assistance Board, 'Homeless Single People',
HMSO, 1966.

30 Crisis at Christmas, Annual fund-raising document,
1976. See also 'Residential Care', Vol. 1, no. 2,
December 1972, for a similar statement.

31 Gill Diamond, Alone with no home - a research study
of some homeless young people in central London in
1970, duplicated, After Six, 1975.

CHAPTER 3 THE RESEARCH ARENA: PARTICIPANTS, SETTINGS,
PERSPECTIVES AND METHODS

1 Stuart Rees, No more than contact, 'British Journal of
Social Work', Vol. 4, no. 3, Autumn 1974.
2 Abraham Maslow, 'The Farther Reaches of Human Nature',
Pelican, 1973, p. 5.
3 Derek Phillips, 'Knowledge from What? - Theories and
Methods in Social Research', Rand McNally, 1971,
p. 141.
4 Derek Phillips, 'Abandoning Method', Jossey Bass,
1973, p. 163.

CHAPTER 4 DIFFERING PERSPECTIVES

1 Peter Archard, Sad, bad or mad - society's confused
response to the skid row alcoholic, in R. Bailey and
J. Youngs, eds, 'Contemporary Social Problems in
Britain', Saxon Lexington, 1973.
2 Dr E.O. Lewis, Appendix One in 'Relief of the Casual
Poor', HMSO, Cmd 3640, XVIII, 121 (1930).
3 Quoted in Stuart Rees, How misunderstanding occurs,
in R. Bailey and Mike Brake, eds, 'Radical Social
Work', Arnold, 1975, p. 74.
4 Herschel Prins, Motivation in social work, 'Social
Work Today', 18 April 1974.

CHAPTER 9 CONCLUSION

1 David Brandon, 'Guidelines to Research in Homelessness', Christian Action, 1972.
2 Steve Billcliffe (compiler), 'Where Homelessness means
Hopelessness', Shelter, 1978.
3 Jane Morton, Who'll house the single?, 'New Society',
25 March 1976.
4 For example, Ted Perry and Dave Burnham, The Mansfield
Homelessness Project, 'Social Work Today', 29 November
1977.
5 Department of Employment, Unemployment rates by age,
'Department of Employment Gazette', June 1977, pp.
718-19.
6 John Hughes, Employ the young, 'New Society', 14
October 1976.

7   David Robins and Philip Cohen, 'Knuckle Sandwich',
    Penguin, 1978, p. 9.
8   Alistair and Gabrielle Cox, 'Borderlines: a partial
    view of detached work with homeless young people',
    National Youth Bureau, 1977.
9   See for further illustration Steven Segal, Jim Baumohl
    and Elsie Johnson, Falling through the cracks:
    mental disorder and social margin in a young vagrant
    population, 'Social Problems', 1977, pp. 387-400.
10 Peter Archard, Sad, mad or bad - society's confused
    response to the skid row alcoholic, in R. Bailey and
    J. Youngs, eds, 'Contemporary Social Problems in
    Britain', Saxon Lexington, 1973, p. 140.
11 Peter L. Berger, 'Pyramids of Sacrifice: Political
    ethics and social change', Penguin, 1977, p. 220.
12 Thomas Rintoul, 'No Room?', Voluntary Hostels Confer-
    ence, 1963.
13 Peter L. Berger, 'Pyramids of Sacrifice', p. 36.

INDEX